Transnational Equity Analysis

Wiley Finance Series

Investment Risk Management
Yen Yee Chong

Understanding International Bank Risk
Andrew Fight

Global Credit Management: An Executive Summary
Ron Wells

Currency Overlay
Neil Record

Fixed Income Strategy: A Practitioner's Guide to Riding the Curve
Tamara Mast Henderson

Active Investment Management
Charles Jackson

Option Theory
Peter James

The Simple Rules of Risk: Revisiting the Art of Risk Management
Erik Banks

Capital Asset Investment: Strategy, Tactics and Tools
Anthony F. Herbst

Brand Assets
Tony Tollington

Swaps and other Derivatives
Richard Flavell

Currency Strategy: A Practitioner's Guide to Currency Trading, Hedging and Forecasting
Callum Henderson

The Investor's Guide to Economic Fundamentals
John Calverley

Measuring Market Risk
Kevin Dowd

An Introduction to Market Risk Management
Kevin Dowd

Behavioural Finance
James Montier

Asset Management: Equities Demystified
Shanta Acharya

An Introduction to Capital Markets: Products, Strategies, Participants
Andrew M. Chisholm

Hedge Funds: Myths and Limits
François-Serge Lhabitant

The Manager's Concise Guide to Risk
Jihad S. Nader

Securities Operations: A Guide to Trade and Position Management
Michael Simmons

Modeling, Measuring and Hedging Operational Risk
Marcelo Cruz

Monte Carlo Methods in Finance
Peter Jäckel

Building and Using Dynamic Interest Rate Models
Ken Kortanek and Vladimir Medvedev

Structured Equity Derivatives: The Definitive Guide to Exotic Options and Structured Notes
Harry Kat

Advanced Modelling in Finance Using Excel and VBA
Mary Jackson and Mike Staunton

Operational Risk: Measurement and Modelling
Jack King

Advanced Credit Risk Analysis: Financial Approaches and Mathematical Models to Assess, Price and Manage Credit Risk
Didier Cossin and Hugues Pirotte

Risk Management and Analysis vol. 1: Measuring and Modelling Financial Risk
Carol Alexander (ed.)

Risk Management and Analysis vol. 2: New Markets and Products
Carol Alexander (ed.)

Transnational Equity Analysis

Mark Clatworthy

John Wiley & Sons, Ltd

Telephone (+44) 1243 779777

Email (for orders and customer service enquiries): cs-books@wiley.co.uk
Visit our Home Page on www.wileyeurope.com or www.wiley.com

Other Wiley Editorial Offices

John Wiley & Sons Inc., 111 River Street, Hoboken, NJ 07030, USA

Jossey-Bass, 989 Market Street, San Francisco, CA 94103-1741, USA

Wiley-VCH Verlag GmbH, Boschstr. 12, D-69469 Weinheim, Germany

John Wiley & Sons Australia Ltd, 33 Park Road, Milton, Queensland 4064, Australia

John Wiley & Sons (Asia) Pte Ltd, 2 Clementi Loop #02-01, Jin Xing Distripark, Singapore 129809

John Wiley & Sons Canada Ltd, 22 Worcester Road, Etobicoke, Ontario, Canada M9W 1L1

Wiley also publishes its books in a variety of electronic formats. Some content that appears in print may not be available in electronic books.

British Library Cataloguing in Publication Data

A catalogue record for this book is available from the British Library

ISBN 0-470-86126-6

Typeset in 10.5/12.5pt Times by TechBooks, New Delhi, India
Printed and bound in Great Britain by Antony Rowe Ltd, Chippenham, Wiltshire.
This book is printed on acid-free paper responsibly manufactured from sustainable forestry in which at least two trees are planted for each one used for paper production.

To the memory of John Goodchild

Contents

Acknowledgements

I am indebted to a number of people who have provided much-appreciated assistance and support during the writing of this book.

First and foremost, I must acknowledge the late John Goodchild, who originally suggested that I write this book. John took a keen interest in the progress of the manuscript from the outset and without him this book would not have been written. It is therefore dedicated to John's memory.

I am especially grateful for the contribution of the investment analysts and fund managers who gave their valuable time to participate in the research, particularly those involved in the interview study. I would also like to thank the (then) Institute of Investment Management and Research (IIMR) for their assistance. In particular, I am grateful for the cooperation of Sir David Dobson and Clive Callow, and for the comments of David Damant.

Many colleagues at Cardiff Business School provided insightful comments on this book at various stages. In particular, I am indebted to Mike Jones for his guidance and support during the empirical study, and to Malcolm Beyron, Roy Chandler, Alpa Dhanani, Barry Morse, Mike Peel and Jill Solomon for their constructive advice. I would also like to acknowledge Professors Vivien Beattie (Glasgow University) and Claire Marston (Heriot-Watt University) for their helpful suggestions on the research.

I am very grateful for the invaluable assistance during the publication process provided by Rachael Wilkie and Chris Swain from John Wiley and Sons. I would also like to extend my gratitude to BASF A.G. for allowing the reproduction of financial statement data. Last, but not least, I would like to thank my family for their much appreciated support during the writing of this book, especially my wife Sally and daughter Holly May.

1 Introduction

1.1 AIMS AND SCOPE OF THE BOOK

Over recent decades, various factors, including technological advances and economic liberalisation, have combined to make equity markets international, rather than national, in scope. Companies are increasingly venturing overseas in search of new, and often less expensive, sources of capital by listing their securities on foreign stock exchanges. Simultaneously, investors are increasingly inclined to diversify internationally in order to benefit from new investment opportunities and to reduce portfolio risk. The economic advantages of this trend to issuers and providers of capital therefore look set to ensure that the importance of national boundaries in finance will continue to diminish.

This internationalisation has been accompanied by a significant growth in the levels of institutional investment in developed stock markets. The majority of shares of large quoted companies are now held by financial institutions such as pension funds, investment trusts and insurance companies. No country illustrates this better than the UK, where private ownership of equities has fallen from over 50% to around 15% since the early 1960s (Myners, 2001).

Despite these parallel trends, comparatively little is known about how financial institutions, particularly fund mangers and investment analysts, discriminate between investment opportunities when faced with a global universe of companies to choose from. Although there is a wealth of evidence on the techniques and sources of information used in domestic equity analysis (e.g., Lee and Tweedie, 1981; Arnold and Moizer, 1984; Pike *et al.*, 1993; Barker, 1998), there is a distinct lack of knowledge of such issues in a transnational context.

This would not be important if national boundaries were as irrelevant in accounting and financial reporting as they are in finance. For various historical, political and economic reasons, accounting systems differ significantly internationally. For example, equity shareholders are not the intended main users of accounting information in certain countries; consequently, financial statements are orientated towards the needs of creditors and/or the government. Furthermore, the fact that financial statements are used principally for taxation purposes in some countries often induces systematic conservatism in reported figures; in such instances, the decision usefulness objective of accounting information is subordinated in order to reduce tax liabilities. Ultimately, of course, international differences in financial reporting systems manifest themselves in the widespread variation in the methods of accounting for specific items such as research and development, depreciation, derivatives, goodwill and consolidation.

The main aim of this book is to assess the impact of national boundaries on institutional investors' equity decision making. In particular, it seeks to examine whether international differences in accounting and financial reporting cause fund managers and investment analysts to adopt different approaches and/or rely on different sources of information when analysing overseas equities compared to domestic (UK) equities. For example, does international accounting diversity foster the use of analysis techniques that avoid non-comparable financial statement information? Do fund managers and analysts rely less on the annual reports of overseas companies due to their unfamiliarity with foreign accounting standards? Are any mechanisms in place to assist institutional investors when deciding whether to buy, hold or sell the shares of foreign firms?

While these questions make transnational equity analysis an interesting subject *per se*, the international harmonisation of accounting standards means that this issue assumes even greater significance. The International Accounting Standards Board (IASB) has been striving to reduce international accounting diversity by promulgating a globally acceptable set of accounting standards which will enhance the cross-border comparability of financial statements. As pointed out by Hopwood (1994), however, much of the discussion of harmonisation is conducted on the basis of *assumptions* of how accounting and other information sources are used in transnational equity investment decisions. Furthermore, there is very little evidence on institutional investors' views of the international harmonisation of accounting.

Prima facie, users of accounting information such as investment analysts and fund managers would appear to be naturally supportive of a process that improves the international comparability of financial statements. However, there is not universal agreement in the academic literature that harmonisation is either necessary or worthwhile. Additionally, some commentators have interpreted analysts' and fund managers' lack of involvement in the harmonisation debate as indicative of indifference; others have gone further in suggesting that this is symptomatic of their interest in maintaining the status quo because international accounting diversity creates a larger market in financial analysis (Hopwood, 1994).

Through a review of the relevant academic literature, and an empirical study of UK-based fund managers and investment analysts, this book seeks to address the issues outlined above. The objectives of the study are:

(i) to examine the relative usefulness of the various analysis techniques used in transnational equity investment decisions;
(ii) to investigate the utility of accounting information and other information sources in transnational equity analysis;
(iii) to assess the impact of international accounting differences on fund managers' and analysts' decision making; and
(iv) to examine the views of analysts and fund managers who are engaged in transnational equity analysis on the international harmonisation of accounting standards.

The findings indicate that the diminution in importance of geographic and national boundaries is increasingly reflected in the ways in which financial institutions are organised. The number of analysts involved exclusively in domestic analysis is apparently declining as analysts who have traditionally followed only UK companies are adopting pan-European focus. Furthermore, institutional investors are increasingly specialising by industrial sector, rather than geographic regions. International comparability of financial statements is therefore likely to become more important over time.

The results also demonstrate that, as has been found in prior research into domestic equity analysis, fundamental analysis is by far the most influential technique used to analyse overseas shares. Consistent with this, accounting information and the annual report are considered very useful by UK analysts and investors in the analysis of domestic and foreign equities. Hence, international differences in accounting and financial reporting do not appear to be significant enough to cause reliance on analysis techniques that avoid the use of accounting information.

In addition to accounting information, direct company contact in the form of meetings with management and company visits is a vital information source to both analysts and fund managers, despite the obvious geographic barriers. In this context, locally-based analysts represent an important interface between overseas companies and UK fund managers. These analysts also assist fund managers in the interpretation of transnational accounting information.

A further finding from the research is that although they do not perceive their decisions to be significantly affected by international accounting differences, both fund managers and analysts are highly supportive of the harmonisation process. This support is attributable to perceived improvements in international comparability and in the quality of measurement and disclosure standards. In addition to reliance on locally-based analysts, UK institutional investors cope with the current international accounting diversity by using less inclusive measures of profits (i.e., earnings before interest, taxation, depreciation and amortisation – EBITDA) and by imposing a risk premium on companies who use financial statements prepared using accounting standards that are unfamiliar or perceived as unreliable.

The two main intentions of the book are: i) to bring the previous academic work in this increasingly important area to a non-academic audience; and ii) to disseminate the main findings of the empirical study. Much of the literature is technical in nature and the findings of such research often do not reach beyond the academic communities working in specialist fields. Moreover, during the research, it became apparent that there was widespread interest in the findings by the analysts and fund managers involved. It is therefore hoped that *inter alia*, the book will be of interest to investment professionals involved in the area of transnational equity analysis. The book may also be of interest to advanced undergraduate and postgraduate students of international financial statement analysis.

1.2 OUTLINE OF THE BOOK

The remainder of the book is organised as follows. Chapters 2 to 5 comprise a review of the previous relevant research. Chapter 2 discusses in more detail the increasing internationalisation of global equity markets and the growing importance of investment analysts and institutional investors. Chapter 3 describes the diversity in international accounting and financial reporting systems and examines their effects on international investors. Chapter 4 reviews the research into domestic analysis techniques, while Chapter 5 completes the literature review by discussing the information sources used in equity analysis.

Chapters 6 to 9 describe how the research was conducted and present the results. Chapter 6 presents the data collection and analysis methods used in the research; then the following three chapters present the results. Chapter 7 examines the analysis techniques used by analysts and fund managers in domestic and transnational equity analysis, while Chapter 8 focuses on the information sources used to analyse UK and overseas shares. Chapter 9 then presents the findings on the views of analysts and fund managers on international accounting diversity and harmonisation.

Chapter 10 concludes the book with a summary of the findings, together with a discussion of the limitations and implications of the study.

1.3 REFERENCES

Arnold, J. and Moizer, P. (1984). 'A survey of the methods used by UK investment analysts to appraise investments in ordinary shares.' *Accounting and Business Research,* **Summer**, 195–207.

Barker, R.G. (1998). 'The market for information: evidence from finance directors, analysts and fund managers.' *Accounting and Business Research*, **29** (1), 1–20.

Hopwood, A.G. (1994). 'Some reflections on "The Harmonization of Accounting Within the EU".' *The European Accounting Review*, **3** (2), 241–253.

Lee, T.A. and Tweedie, D.P. (1981). *The Institutional Investor and Financial Information.* The Institute of Chartered Accountants in England and Wales, London.

Myners, P. (2001). *Institutional Investment in the UK: A Review*, H.M. Treasury, London.

Pike, R., Meerjanssen, J. and Chadwick, L. (1993). 'The appraisal of ordinary shares by investment analysts in the UK and Germany.' *Accounting and Business Research*, **23** (92), 489–499.

2
The Internationalisation of Equity Markets and Growth in Institutional Investment

2.1 INTRODUCTION

Although the offer for sale of company shares to overseas investors can be traced back at least as far as the 17th century, recent decades have seen the most dramatic rise in the internationalisation of global equity markets. Finance theory demonstrates that transnational investment holds significant advantages for both investors and companies. Investors are able to obtain risk reductions through international portfolio diversification; this is especially germane to the UK which is widely viewed as the most internationally orientated of the major financial centres. In addition, various benefits may accrue to companies as a result of listing on foreign stock exchanges. Such benefits include a lower cost of equity capital and increased corporate recognition. Given the benefits that both providers and recipients of capital can obtain from this internationalisation, the trend is set to continue.

The growing internationalisation of global capital markets has been paralleled by the increasing importance of institutional investors on major international stock exchanges. Levels of institutional investment are particularly high on the London Stock Exchange, where over three quarters of the total market value is owned by financial institutions. Other major international stock markets, such as the US, Japan and Germany are also characterised by increasing institutionalisation. For example, in the US, between 1946 and 1996, holdings of US equities by pension funds, insurance companies, mutual funds and other institutions grew from 6% to 50% (Brown, 1998).

These parallel trends of increasing institutional investment and the escalating propensity to invest across national boundaries provide the context for the remainder of this book. The internationalisation of equity markets has led to large institutional investors being increasingly required to analyse the securities of foreign firms. The processes involved in these analyses, together with associated investment decisions, form the principal focus of the book.

The remainder of this chapter highlights the increase in activity in the trading of securities of foreign firms on the world's major stock exchanges, paying particular attention to the UK market. It continues by describing the increase in institutional investment in global equity markets.

2.2 THE GROWTH IN TRADE OF FOREIGN SECURITIES

The trading of the shares of foreign companies on organised exchanges is by no means a new phenomenon. Davis *et al.* (2003) discuss the development of overseas equity investment, tracing the roots of foreign shareholdings back to the early 17th century in Amsterdam. Here, the United East India Company (or Vereenigde Oost-indische Compagnie) was keen to attract foreign shareholders to finance its trading in the East Indies. The Bank of England was among a number of other British joint-stock companies which issued shares to both domestic and foreign investors at the turn of the 18th century; but it was in the late 1800s that foreign listings of non-governmental corporations took place.[1] Some interesting statistics for the early 20th century are provided by Morgan and Thomas (1969). They estimate the holdings of publicly issued overseas securities in 1913 to be over £3,700 million; of this, approximately 50% was invested in the colonies, 20% in the US and Latin America and 15% in Europe, indicating a significant degree of geographic dispersion. Hence, even at this time, the London Stock Exchange was unrivalled in the extent to which it attracted the securities of foreign governments and companies, particularly when compared to New York (Michie, 1987).

After the first World War, London conceded its position of dominance to the New York Stock Exchange and the number of overseas listings waned during the mid 20th Century. Table 2.1 contains data from the London Stock Exchange as at the end of December 2000, and provides an indication of the temporal listing patterns of international companies in London.[2] The earliest remaining foreign company to list in London is the St Lawrence & Ottawa Railway Co. in 1876; in the subsequent 84 years to 1960, only 44 foreign companies listed. After the 1960s, however, a resurgent growth in foreign companies listing took place in each decade, with the number of listings doubling from the 1960s through to the end of the century. The past two decades have been particularly important in attracting foreign companies

[1] Davis *et al.* (2003, p. 125) illustrate this point with the example of the shares placed on the Amsterdam stock market in 1854 by the Illinois Central rail company, which was forced to use the Dutch (rather than London) exchange to raise funds due to the financial demands of the Crimean War on the London market.

[2] Clearly, these figures are indicative in nature since they only record the listing patterns of those international companies which are currently listed on the London Stock Exchange. They are therefore potentially subject to a 'survivorship bias', as they ignore those listed companies which have subsequently left the stock market.

Table 2.1 Temporal listing patterns of international companies on the London Stock Exchange

	Number of international companies listing	
Time period	Number	%
Pre-1960	44	8.8
1961–1970	20	4.0
1971–1980	57	11.4
1981–1990	125	25.0
1991–2000	251	50.1
Undated	4	0.8
Total	501	100

to list their securities in London, emphasising the growing significance of transnational investment in recent years.

It is also worth noting that this phenomenon is not confined to the UK. As shown in Table 2.2, with the exception of the Tokyo Stock Exchange, the world's largest stock markets each accommodates a significant number of foreign companies. The data in Table 2.2 also demonstrate the continuing international dominance of the London Stock Exchange in raising overseas capital, where foreign companies represent over a fifth of the total number of companies listed.

London's reputation as a key international financial centre is also reinforced by the value of foreign companies listed on the Official List, compared to the value of UK companies. Table 2.3 shows that the market capitalisation of foreign (international listed) companies was 170% of the value of UK companies at the end of December 2001. Furthermore, the figures in Table 2.3 demonstrate that foreign companies are active in raising capital

Table 2.2 Foreign and domestic companies listed on major exchanges as at 31/12/99

	London		NASDAQ		NYSE		Tokyo	
	No.	%	No.	%	No.	%	No.	%
Domestic companies	1,945	79.6	4,400	91.1	2,187	84.4	1,889	97.8
Foreign companies	499	20.4	429	8.9	405	15.6	43	2.2
Total	2,444	100	4,829	100	2,592	100	1,932	100

Sources: IASB web-site and London Stock Exchange (1999).

Table 2.3 UK and international companies on the London Stock Exchange

	UK listed	International listed
Equity market value (£bn)	1,147.8	1,901.7
Total equity raised in 2002 (£m)	16,424.3	5,455.2
Total funds raised in 2002 (£m)	125,915.0	81,704.9

Source: London Stock Exchange (2002a).

on the London Stock Exchange, as almost £5.5 billion of equity capital was raised by foreign companies in the London primary market during 2002, relative to just over £16 billion for UK listed firms. Hence, it appears that these companies are listing their securities in London for more than just public relations reasons.

Although data on foreign listings can provide a useful guide to activity in the trade in overseas equities, they do not present the whole picture. In addition to the companies listed on London Stock Exchange, UK institutional investors also play a significant role in the dealing of overseas firms' securities on foreign stock markets. For example, in 2002, the total value of business conducted in foreign equities by London Stock Exchange member firms was £218 billion – 83% more than the value of turnover in UK equities (London Stock Exchange, 2002b).

2.3 DETERMINANTS OF THE INTERNATIONALISATION OF EQUITY MARKETS

Given the patterns of increasing levels of equity capital crossing national boundaries discussed above, an interesting question arises: what lies beneath this trend? This question can be addressed both to those seeking to attract capital (i.e., companies on the capital 'demand side') and to those investors who provide capital (i.e., capital supply side).

2.3.1 Capital demand-side factors

2.3.1.1 Motives for foreign stock exchange listings

Underlying the internationalisation of equity markets are various motivational factors for companies seeking listings of their securities on foreign exchanges. Tondkar *et al.* (1989) found that one of the key attractions of foreign listings is the ability of companies to reduce their cost of capital. This can be achieved by reaching a wider investor base, thus providing access to more liquid, integrated markets (Radebaugh *et al.*, 1995). The increased investor recognition resulting from listing on foreign exchanges has also been shown to reduce the cost of capital (Baker *et al.*, 1999; Merton, 1987). In line with these arguments, Doidge *et al.* (2004) find that overseas companies that cross-list their shares in the US are valued up to 37% higher than their domestic counterparts without such a listing.

A further incentive for listing on developed stock markets is that the capital requirements of large multinational companies can often exceed the supply of domestic funds, particularly in countries where stock markets are relatively under-developed, or where equity has not traditionally been the primary source of finance. For example, in 1992, activity in the shares of Daimler Benz (now Daimler Chrysler) constituted 11.5% of the total turnover on all German exchanges (Radebaugh *et al.*, 1995). The company had effectively outgrown the supply of funds available in its domestic market. This was at least partly why Daimler Benz sought a listing on the New York Stock Exchange in 1993.

Listing on foreign exchanges also provides companies with opportunities to raise their international profile, thus increasing the marketability of their securities and, in some cases, their products. Baker *et al.* (1999) found evidence that international cross-listings can improve corporate visibility, as analyst coverage (i.e., the number of analysts covering the company) and media attention increased after the listing. By raising capital to finance foreign operations in the local market, multinational companies are also able to reduce foreign currency exposure, reduce reliance on domestic capital supplies and possibly improve political relations with hosts governments (Saudagaran and Biddle, 1991).

In an investigation of the association between benefits from foreign listings and firm specific characteristics, Rees (1998) found that increased corporate visibility and enhanced capital raising opportunities do not necessarily occur in all cases. He provides evidence that firms benefit more if they are able to expand their operations in the foreign market, through increased corporate visibility, growth and public relations.

2.3.1.2 Costs of foreign stock exchange listings

Although existing evidence demonstrates that the benefits of dual listings are material for many companies, they are not achievable without costs. Most obvious in this context are the direct listing costs and the associated financial costs of accounting and legal expertise. These arise as a result of the often rigorous regulatory and disclosure requirements with which companies must comply on major stock exchanges. These costs are particularly pronounced on US stock markets, where the regulations set out by the Securities and Exchange Commission (SEC) are the most onerous of all major markets. Foreign companies listed in the US are required to prepare reconciliations of financial statements according to US generally accepted accounting principles (GAAP) if the figures are materially different, which can often involve substantial costs. These requirements are reported to have led to disputes regarding the validity of Daimler Benz's accounting figures due to the substantial differences reported between German GAAP and US GAAP (Flower, 1997).

In line with these arguments, Saudagaran and Biddle (1995) found a significant inverse relationship between foreign listings and the level of disclosure requirements on the foreign exchange, suggesting that high regulatory requirements act as a significant deterrent to overseas companies. Yamori and Baba (2001) found similar results for Japanese firms. Their survey evidence showed that even though Japanese managers are aware of the benefits arising from foreign listings, disclosure and reporting requirements are the most significant obstacle to overseas listings.

A further cost associated with foreign listings is that a 'flowback' of companies' shares can occur. This is where the securities listed on the foreign exchange make their way back to owners in the company's country of domicile as a result of different levels of supply and demand between domestic and foreign stock markets. The effect of this can be to increase the supply of the securities from the foreign stock exchange, resulting in a depressed domestic share price – a phenomenon observed with British Telecom shares in the 1980s (Tondkar *et al.*, 1989).

Although the above evidence suggests that companies consider the regulatory and disclosure requirements of foreign stock exchanges burdensome, the growth in cross-listings over recent years indicates that the benefits of a foreign listing are perceived to be greater. In fact, research has demonstrated that companies often voluntarily disclose levels of information which exceed those required by the host stock exchange. For example, Meek and Gray (1989) studied voluntary disclosures by companies from France, Holland, Sweden and Germany listed on the London Stock Exchange. They matched a list of the relevant requirements against the actual disclosures relating to issues such as forecasting, segmental information, research and development and financial trend data, and found that most companies exceeded a wide range of these requirements across the four countries. This appears to militate against the argument of companies being deterred from foreign listings by the disclosure regulations. However, more recent evidence suggests that companies benefit from increased disclosure in the form of a reduction in the cost of capital (Botosan, 1997; Leuz and Verrecchia, 2000).

2.3.2 Capital supply-side factors

2.3.2.1 Portfolio theory and international diversification

One of the most compelling arguments for investment in overseas securities is provided by modern portfolio theory. Given certain assumptions, this theory posits that investors can benefit (at no incremental cost) from diversification, relative to holding single securities. This is because it is possible to achieve reductions in risk, while maintaining a given level of return. These gains arise as a result of imperfect or negative correlations between returns on investments. The closer the correlation between investments is to −1, the greater are the opportunities for reductions in portfolio risk.

The roots of portfolio theory lie in the seminal paper by Markowitz (1952), who realised that simply focusing on the maximisation of security returns predicts that investors would place all their funds in the security with the highest expected return – and therefore offers no explanation for why investors hold diversified portfolios. Markowitz went on to propose that rational investors consider both security returns and the variation in these returns when deciding where to place their funds; i.e., returns should be maximised *and* variance in returns should be minimised. This analysis demonstrates that while the returns of a portfolio are a weighted-average of the returns of the individual securities, the variability of returns is always lower than the weighted-average risk of the individual securities (provided that the returns are not perfectly positively correlated). The variance of the portfolio therefore depends on three factors: the degree of correlation between the returns on the securities; the individual variance of each security in the portfolio; and finally, the proportion of the portfolio invested in each security. Opportunities for risk reductions increase (albeit at a diminishing marginal rate) as the number of imperfectly correlated securities in a portfolio increases, due to the impact of covariance between the securities in the portfolio.

The limit to diversification is the constant level of risk that represents systematic risk. Unlike firm-specific (i.e., unsystematic risk), systematic risk cannot be diversified away. Rational investors will want to eliminate unsystematic risk by holding the market portfolio which comprises all securities in the market. The incentive to invest in overseas securities arises because investment in domestic portfolios only reduces risk to the level of systematic risk on the domestic stock market. If the returns to securities of firms in different industries within a country move together, greater reductions in risk can be achieved by diversifying portfolios internationally, i.e., a lower level of systematic risk can be attained by investing in an internationally diversified portfolio relative to that of a purely domestic portfolio, without forfeiting returns.

These arguments are not purely theoretical; the benefits of international diversification have been demonstrated empirically by a large number of authors. Grubel (1968) was the first to adapt the analysis of Markowitz (1952) to the international setting. He provided empirical evidence that US investors could achieve higher rates of return or lower portfolio variances by diversifying their portfolios across 11 other industrialised countries. More specifically, using *ex post* stock market returns data, Grubel calculated that investors could have achieved an annual return of 12.6% on a portfolio diversified across all 11 countries for the same level of variability found in a US portfolio, which would have generated 7.5% (i.e., diversification resulted in an increase in returns of 68% for the same level of risk).

In an extension of this analysis to 28 countries, Levy and Sarnat (1970) showed that over the period 1951–1967, even though US equities performed relatively well and the risk (standard deviation of returns to national indices) was low relative to other countries in their analysis, American investors would still have benefited from international diversification. The results of Levy and Sarnat's analysis appeared *prima facie* to be counter intuitive, as they advocated the investment in countries that had relatively low returns in order to reduce the variance of the overall portfolio. For example, they point out (p. 671):

> Perhaps the most striking feature of the composition of the diversified international portfolios is the relatively high proportion of investments in developing or borderline countries such as Venezuela, South Africa, New Zealand, Mexico and Japan. Depending on the interest rate assumed, the proportion of such investments accounts for about 40 to 60 percent of the aggregate portfolio.

Further surprising results included the virtual exclusion of developed Western European countries from optimal portfolios and a weighting of around 20% for Japan, which by itself had the third most volatile returns. Levy and Sarnat's findings demonstrate the high import of the covariance between securities relative to the variance of the individual variances, particularly as the portfolio grows in size. Hence, the reason why Japan received such a high weighting was due to the negative or very low correlation between the Japanese index and the other indices in the portfolio. Similarly, the economies of the then European Common Market were excluded largely due to their relatively high positive correlation with the United States.

In an important study, which compared the risk and return characteristics of domestic and international portfolios, Solnik (1974) found that with as few as 40 securities, by diversifying internationally and creating a portfolio containing equal proportions of major US and European stock markets, a

US investor could reduce the risk (for no loss of return) of a purely domestic portfolio by more than half. This relationship is illustrated in Figure 2.1.

An important point to note is that reductions in risk resulting from international diversification rely on imperfect correlations between the returns on international stock markets. An internationally diversified portfolio is substantially less risky than a purely domestic one because stock returns display lower positive correlation across countries than within a country. Numerous studies provide empirical evidence of this effect (e.g., Levy and Sarnat, 1970; Solnik, 1974; Liljeblom *et al.*, 1997). The evidence on recent correlations between international markets, however, is mixed, with some suggesting that the degree of correlation is increasing between markets (e.g., Arshanapalli and Doukas, 1993; Longin and Solnik, 1995). Notwithstanding this, the degree of integration is sufficiently low so as to still permit significant reduction in risk from international diversification (e.g., Ibbotson and Wang, 2000). Interestingly, Heaney *et al.* (2001) suggest that international stock markets have become regionally integrated, possibly as a result of trading blocs and intra-regional macroeconomic cooperation, such as the European Union (EU) and the Association of Southeast Asian

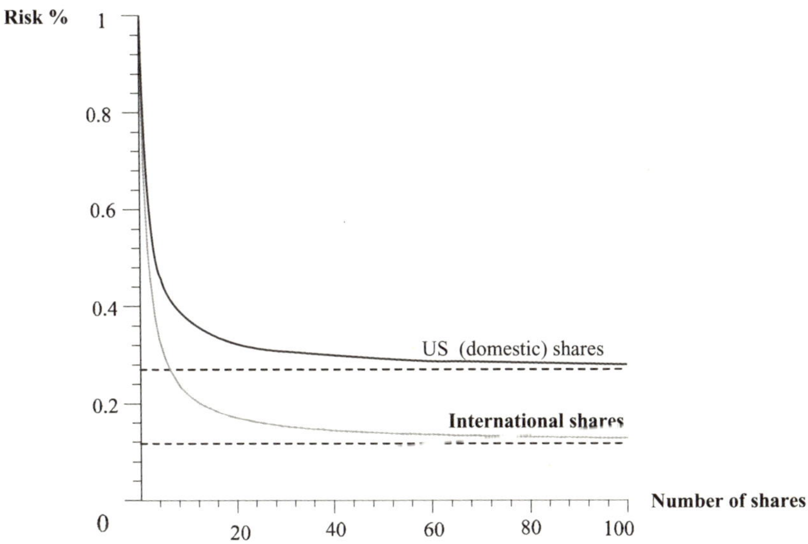

Figure 2.1 Benefits of diversifying internationally (Solnik 1974)

Nations (ASEAN). Accordingly, Heaney and Hooper recommend that investors diversify outside regions rather than outside countries.

Against this background of increasing integration of international markets, recent research is focusing on the benefits of diversification across industries rather than countries. Ehling and Ramos (2003) examine the European Union countries before, during and after the convergence period and find that diversification based on country *and* industry portfolios is superior, although a country-based strategy in itself is not preferable to an industry-based strategy.

Despite the well-documented benefits from international diversification, the take-up of international investments has been relatively slow.[3] A significant 'home bias' therefore exists, particularly in the US market (e.g., French and Poterba, 1991; Coval and Moskowitz 1999). This home bias 'puzzle' has been partially attributed to information asymmetries arising from foreign investors being less well-informed than domestic investors (e.g., Gehrig, 1993; Kang and Stulz, 1997; Brennan and Cao, 1997). Frost and Pownall (2000) provide evidence of such asymmetries. They find that companies disclose information unequally between local and foreign investors, even though this often contravenes stock market requirements. However, Brennan and Cao (1997) speculate that information asymmetries may be weaker for financial institutions.

In summary, the literature demonstrates that because of the benefits both to companies and investors, equity markets have become increasingly internationalised in recent years. Moreover, due to the significant levels of funds still held in domestic funds, the trend is set to continue. The following section examines the increasing involvement and importance of institutional investors, which has accompanied the growth in institutional investment on major stock markets.

2.4 THE GROWTH IN INSTITUTIONAL INVESTMENT

2.4.1 The importance of institutional investment

Institutional investors play an increasingly important role in most developed stock markets, including Canada, Germany, Japan, South Africa and the US. Few countries, however, have levels of institutional ownership and influence to match those in the UK, which has the highest proportion (65% in 1998)

[3] Evidence suggests that US investors are becoming more internationally orientated. For example, Ogden (1997) reports that in 1992 allocation to non-US securities in US corporate pension funds averaged 7.9% which increased to 9%, 9.5%, 10.1% and 10.8% in 1993, 1994, 1995 and 1996 respectively.

of institutional assets held in equities (OECD, 2000). The Myners Report on institutional investment in the UK (Myners, 2001) documents the reduction in individual share ownership, which has fallen from 50% of the market in the early 1960s to under 20% at the present time.

Table 2.4 reports figures for the growth in institutional ownership of UK equities over the period 1963 to 1998 and shows a substantial rate of growth in institutional ownership from 29 to 52.3%, and a simultaneous decline in individual ownership, from 54 to 16.7%. In addition, while the proportion of equity held by institutions fell between 1989 and 1998, this was attributable to a growth in holdings by foreign investors (from 12.8 to 27.6%) rather than individual holdings, which fell from 20.6 to 16.7%.

Although traditionally seen as the bastion of the private investor, institutional investors are also becoming increasingly important equity holders in the US, where the proportion of institutional investors' ownership of the top companies is already around 60%. Bricker and Chandar (2000) argue that the traditional view understates the historical significance of institutional investors in the US. They provide evidence that investment banks played a key role in the investment in, and control of, large companies in the early twentieth century. Bricker and Chandar point out that due to institutional investors' ability to mobilise large amounts of capital (via their control of bank deposits and insurance funds) these institutions were 'pivotal' in the development of early capital markets.

Financial institutions therefore play a vital role in the stock market and their decisions often have a substantial impact upon the share prices of large

Table 2.4 Percentage of total UK equity owned

	1963	1975	1989	1998
Insurance companies	10.0	15.9	18.6	21.6
Pension funds	6.4	16.8	30.6	21.7
Unit/investment trusts	1.3	4.1	7.5	4.9
Other financial institutions	11.3	10.5	1.1	4.1
Total financial institutions	*29*	*47.3*	*57.8*	*52.3*
Rest of the World	7.0	5.6	12.8	27.6
Charities	2.1	2.3	2.3	1.4
Private non-financial firms	5.1	3.0	3.8	1.4
Public sector	1.5	3.6	2.0	0.1
Banks	1.3	0.7	0.7	0.6
Individuals	54.0	37.5	20.6	16.7
Total	100	100	100	100

Source: Office for National Statistics (2000).

and medium-sized public companies. Their increasing dominance means that they are among the most important users of financial reporting and accounting information. However, these institutions are not a homogeneous group. In the context of equity investment, a distinction can be drawn between fund managers and investment analysts.

2.4.2 The role of fund managers and investment analysts

While fund managers are important users of accounting information in their own right, they are assisted in capital markets by investment analysts (Schipper, 1991). These analysts do not make investments themselves; rather they act as information intermediaries between companies and investors (Moizer and Arnold, 1984). Schipper (1991, p. 106) notes that it may be useful to distinguish between buy-side and sell-side analysts, not least because they may face dissimilar incentives due to the nature of their employers:

> While both make recommendations about which stocks to buy, sell and hold, sell-side analysts are the primary producers of earnings forecasts. Buy-side analysts tend to be employed by money management firms or institutional investors while sell-side analysts tend to be employed at broker/dealer firms that serve institutional investors.

Sell-side analysts provide information on the companies that they follow to institutional investors, particularly to individual fund managers, who ultimately make the investment decision. This information may include recommendations of whether to buy, sell or hold company shares, forecasts of company earnings, and research reports (Michaely and Womack, 1999). The demand for the services of sell-side analysts from fund managers arises from differences in the degree of specialisation between the two groups. Sell-side analysts cover fewer companies, as unlike fund managers, they do not have to spend time constructing and monitoring portfolios. As such, they are able to provide more detailed and comprehensive analyses (Moizer and Arnold, 1984). Fund managers, by contrast, follow a greater number of companies, have to construct and monitor portfolios and thus spend significantly less time than analysts appraising shares.

Recent academic research is beginning to challenge the conventional views of analysts as purely intermediaries and question the independence of analysts' advice to fund managers. Investment banks and brokerage firms (i.e., the employers of sell-side analysts) have three sources of income. These are first, corporate financing, issuance of securities and merger advisory services; second, brokerage services; and finally, proprietary trading (Michaely and Womack, 1999).[4] Analysts must maintain an external reputation in order to add credibility to the reports, recommendations and forecasts that they produce and thus stay employed.[5] However, as Michaely and Womack (1999, p. 654) point out, 'When analysts issue opinions and recommendations about firms that have business dealings with their corporate financing divisions, this conflict may result in recommendations and opinions that are positively biased'. Lin and McNichols (1998) also provide evidence that the recommendations and growth forecasts of analysts affiliated with the company being analysed are significantly more favourable than those of unaffiliated analysts. Increasingly, therefore, the view of analysts as disinterested intermediaries has come under increasing pressure, although most research has been conducted in the US; it is noteworthy, however, that the UK financial regulatory authorities appear to be concerned about this issue following law suits against US financial institutions where analyst independence was jeopardised (FSA, 2002).

2.5 SUMMARY

This chapter has discussed two important trends affecting stock markets over recent decades: increasing internationalisation and growth in institutional investment. Most major stock markets have been affected by these trends, particularly the UK market, which was shown to be the most internationally orientated, and with the highest levels of institutional ownership.

Companies listing on stock markets outside their country of domicile have made a significant contribution to the internationalisation of stock markets. By listing on overseas stock markets, companies may lower their cost of capital and increase recognition of their securities and their products. Investors can also benefit by diversifying their portfolios internationally as theoretical and empirical evidence shows that lower risk can be obtained without sacrificing returns.

This chapter has also highlighted relationships between institutional investors and investment analysts. While early research portrays analysts as intermediaries who synthesise and analyse information from companies before providing advice to fund managers, recent research indicates that analysts must be viewed in light of the motives and revenue sources of their employers, who are keen to attract corporate finance work from the companies being analysed.

---

[4] Note, with the exception of bespoke research, analysis *per se* is not a direct source of income for investment banks and stockbrokers.

[5] For example, see Mikhail *et al.* (1999) for evidence that relative forecast accuracy is important to analysts in this context.

One issue which has important implications for the internationalisation of equity markets is the fact that accounting and financial reporting regimes vary significantly between countries. The analysis and valuation of foreign firms therefore often involves accounting information prepared under different measurement bases and different levels of disclosure. However, over recent years, attempts have been made to reduce international accounting diversity through a process of harmonisation. The research into these issues forms the basis of the following chapter.

2.6 REFERENCES

Arshanapalli, B. and Doukas, J. (1993). 'International stock market linkages: evidence from the pre- and post-1987 period.' *Journal of Banking and Finance*, **17** (1), 193–208.

Baker, H. K., Nafsinger, J. R. and Weaver, D.G. (1999). 'International cross listing and visibility.' *New York Stock Exchange Working Paper*.

Botosan, C.A. (1997). 'Disclosure level and the cost of equity capital.' *The Accounting Review*, **72** (3), 323–349.

Brennan, M. and Cao, H.H. (1997). 'International portfolio investment flows.' *Journal of Finance*, **52** (5), 1851–1880.

Bricker, R. and Chandar, N. (2000). 'Where Berle and Means went wrong: a reassessment of capital market agency and financial reporting.' *Accounting, Organizations and Society*, **25**, 529–554.

Brown, C. (1998). 'Rise of the institutional equity funds: implications for managerialism.' *Journal of Economic Issues*, **32** (3), 803–821.

Coval, J.D. and Moskowitz, T.J. (1999). 'Home bias at home: local equity preference in domestic portfolio choice.' *Journal of Finance*, **54**, 2045–2073.

Davis, L., Neal, L. and White, E.N. (2003). 'How it all began: the rise of listing requirements on the London, Berlin, Paris, and New York stock exchanges.' *International Journal of Accounting*, **38**, 117–143.

Doidge, C., Karolyi, A. and Stulz, R. (2004). 'Why are firms listed in the U.S. worth more?' *Journal of Financial Economics*, **71**, 205–238.

Ehling, P. and Ramos, S.B. (2003). 'Geographical versus industrial diversification: a mean variance spanning approach.' *HEC Lausanne Working Paper*, April 2003.

Flower, J. (1997). 'The future shape of harmonization: the EU versus the IASC versus the SEC.' *The European Accounting Review*, **6** (2), 281–303.

French, K. and Poterba, J.M. (1991). 'Investor diversification and international equity markets.' *American Economic Review*, **81** (2), 222–226.

Frost, C.A. and Pownall, G. (2000). 'Equal access to information: do cross listed firms' stock prices respond to earnings disclosed in overseas and local markets?' *Asia-Pacific Journal of Accounting and Economics*, **7**, 97–127.

FSA (2002). *Investment Research: Conflicts and Other Issues*, Financial Services Authority Discussion Paper, London.

Gehrig, T. (1993). 'An information based explanation of the domestic bias in international equity investment.' *Scandinavian Journal of Economics*, **95** (1), 97–109.

Grubel, H.G. (1968). 'Internationally diversified portfolios: welfare gains and capital flows.' *American Economic Review*, **58** (5), 1299–1314.

Heaney, R., Hooper, V. and Jaugietis, M. (2001). 'Regional integration of national stock markets.' *University of New South Wales Working Paper.*

Ibbotson, R.G. and Wang, C.H. (2000). 'Global asset allocation: philosophy, process, and performance.' *Journal of Investing*, **Spring**, 39–51.

Kang, J. and Stulz, R.M. (1997). 'Why is there a home-bias? An analysis of foreign portfolio equity ownership in Japan.' *Journal of Financial Economics*, **46**, 3–28.

Leuz, C. and Verrecchia, R.E. (2000). 'The economic consequences of increased disclosure.' *Journal of Accounting Research*, **38**, 91–124.

Levy, H. and Sarnat, M. (1970). 'International diversification of investment portfolios.' *American Economic Review*, **60** (4), 668–675.

Liljeblom, E., Loflund, A. and Krokfors, F. (1997). 'The benefits from diversification for Nordic investors.' *Journal of Banking and Finance*, **21**, 469–490.

Lin, H. and McNichols, M.F. (1998). 'Underwriting relationships, analysts' earnings forecasts and investment recommendations.' *Journal of Accounting and Economics*, **25**, 101–127.

London Stock Exchange (1999). *Secondary Market Fact Sheet*, December.

London Stock Exchange (2002a). *Primary Market Fact Sheet*, December.

London Stock Exchange (2002b). *Secondary Market Fact Sheet*, December.

Longin, F. and Solnik, B. (1995). 'Is the correlation in international equity returns constant?' *Journal of International Money and Finance*, **14** (1), 3–26.

Markowitz, H. (1952). 'Portfolio selection.' *Journal of Finance*, **7** (1), 77–91.

Meek, G.K. and Gray, S.J. (1989). 'Globalization of stock markets and foreign listing requirements: voluntary disclosures by continental European companies listed on the London Stock Exchange.' *Journal of International Business Studies*, **Summer**, 315–336.

Merton, R.C. (1987) 'A simple model of capital market equilibrium with incomplete information.' *Journal of Finance*, **42** (3), 483–510.

Michaely, R. and Womack, K.L. (1999). 'Conflict of interest and the credibility of underwriter analyst recommendations.' *The Review of Financial Studies*, **12** (4), 653–686.

Michie, R.C. (1987). *The London and New York Stock Exchanges, 1850–1914*, Allen and Unwin, London.

Mikhail, M.B., Walther, B.R. and Willis, R.H. (1999). 'Does forecast accuracy matter to security analysts?' *Accounting Review*, **74** (2), 185–200.

Moizer, P. and Arnold, J. (1984). 'Share appraisal by investment analysts – portfolio vs. non-portfolio managers.' *Accounting and Business Research*, **Autumn**, 341–348.

Morgan, E.V. and Thomas, W.A. (1969). *The Stock Exchange: its History and its Functions*, 2nd edn, Elek Books, London.

Myners, P. (2001). *Institutional Investment in the UK: A Review*, H.M. Treasury, London.

OECD (2000). *Institutional Investors Statistical Yearbook*, Organization for Economic Co-operation and Development, Paris.

Office for National Statistics (2000). *Share ownership: a report on the ownership of shares at 31st December 1998*. Office for National Statistics, The Stationery Office, London.

Ogden, J. (1997). '10.8% and climbing: US pension funds continue to step up investing abroad.' *Global Finance*, **11** (1), 15–16.

Radebaugh, L.H., Gebhardt, G. and Gray, S.J. (1995). 'Foreign stock exchange listings: a case study of Daimler-Benz.' *Journal of International Financial Management and Accounting*, **6** (2), 158–192.

Rees, L. (1998). 'Realized benefits from foreign listings.' *Journal of International Accounting, Auditing & Taxation*, **7** (1), 1–20.

Saudagaran, S.M. and Biddle, G.C. (1991). 'Foreign stock listings: benefits, costs, and the accounting policy dilemma.' *Accounting Horizons*, **5** (3), 69–80.

Saudagaran, S.M. and Biddle, G.C. (1995). 'Foreign listing location: a study of MNCs and stock exchanges in eight countries.' *Journal of International Business Studies*, **Second Quarter**, 319–341.

Schipper, K. (1991). 'Analysts' forecasts.' *Accounting Horizons*, **December**, 105–121.

Solnik, B. (1974). 'Why not diversify internationally, rather than domestically?' *Financial Analysts Journal*, **July-August**, 48–54.

Tondkar, R.H., Adhikari, A. and Coffman, E.N. (1989). 'The internationalization of equity markets: motivations for foreign corporate listing and filing and listing requirements of five major stock exchanges.' *International Journal of Accounting*, **24**, 143–163.

Yamori, N. and Baba, T. (2001). 'Japanese management views on overseas exchange listings: survey results.' *Journal of International Financial Management and Accounting*, **12** (3), 286–316.

3
International Accounting Diversity and the Harmonisation of International Accounting

3.1 INTRODUCTION

The internationalisation of financial markets described in the previous chapter has served to emphasise the significant variation which exists between national accounting and financial reporting systems. This variation is a product of differences in the importance of the institutional and cultural factors which characterise the national financial reporting environment. Considerable research has been devoted to the identification of such factors; this chapter reviews this research.

Research has also assessed the impact of these international accounting differences upon reported accounting figures and upon stock markets. This chapter reviews this research and describes how international accounting differences are being gradually eroded by harmonisation attempts by regulators, particularly the International Accounting Standards Board (IASB). The implications of international accounting differences for the analysis of financial statements are then reviewed.

3.2 CAUSES OF INTERNATIONAL ACCOUNTING DIFFERENCES

The internationalisation of financial markets has drawn increasing attention to the diversity of national accounting and financial reporting systems. This diversity manifests itself at various levels, from the general institutional characteristics of national financial reporting regimes, through to specific accounting policies. The identification and understanding of determinants of accounting diversity are necessary precursors to harmonisation; research in this area can assist in targeting those areas that will reduce accounting differences and thus enhance the comparability of accounting information most effectively. Moreover, as argued by Gray (1988), international classification differences may be relevant in the promotion of economic integration. It is therefore unsurprising that the causes of international differences have

Table 3.1 Proposed reasons for international accounting differences

1. Nature of business ownership and financing system
2. Colonial inheritance
3. Invasions
4. Taxation
5. Inflation
6. Level of education
7. Age and size of accountancy profession
8. Stage of economic development
9. Legal systems
10. Culture
11. History
12. Geography
13. Language
14. Influence of theory
15. Political systems, social climate
16. Religion
17. Accidents

Source: Nobes (1998) p. 163.

received a great deal of attention in the academic literature. Table 3.1 lists 17 possible reasons for international accounting differences identified by Nobes (1998) from previous research.

Of particular interest in Table 3.1 are business ownership and financing, the type of legal system, taxation and the accounting profession. These factors are typically perceived as the most prominent determinants of accounting differences in the mainstream comparative international accounting literature (e.g., Choi *et al.*, 1999; Nobes and Parker, 2002; Roberts *et al.*, 2002).

3.2.1 Business ownership and financing

As is well known, the relative importance of equity and debt finance varies substantially between countries. The orientation of financial reporting systems therefore differs accordingly. Nobes and Parker (2002) note that within the EU, debt-equity ratios range from 20% (for the UK) to 55% (for Switzerland). In countries where companies are predominantly equity financed, financial reporting systems are characterised by focus on profitability and growth, as a guide to return on invested capital. Moreover, equity finance is normally associated with a divorce of ownership from control. Therefore, investors do not generally have internal access to financial disclosure (although this is changing). Thus, there is a greater demand for comprehensive public disclosure in equity-based systems.

With debt financing, however, fixed returns lead to a focus on companies' ability to meet repayments; consequently, financial reporting is orientated towards creditor protection (Roberts *et al.*, 2002). Furthermore, credit-based financing systems are typically dominated by banks and other financial institutions, rather than market-traded debt. These institutions often have the necessary access to the information they need for their investment decisions. Consequently, public financial disclosure in debt-based countries is generally more limited than in equity-based countries (Choi *et al.*, 1999).

3.2.2 Legal systems

While no two legal systems are identical, the literature on international accounting differences distinguishes between two main types of legal systems: those developed from Romano-Germanic code-law or civil law, and those from English common law (e.g., David and Brierley, 1985; Ball *et al.*, 2000). Although there are variations within the civil law category, civil systems are typically characterised by detailed statutes, where accounting procedures and policies are clearly prescribed (Choi *et al.*, 1999).

Countries whose legal systems are based on common law, by contrast, generally rely on limited statutory prescription and incremental interpretation and application of statutes by the judiciary. Legislation holds the ultimate sanction for breaches of accounting practice, although detailed accounting standards are generally laid out by non-governmental standard setters and authorities. This distinction is becoming increasingly blurred, however, as countries commonly used as exemplars of civil law systems (most notably Germany) have established independent standard-setting authorities. Generally, though, the accounting regulatory environment is more prescriptive and less flexible in civil law countries than in common law countries.

It is sometimes noted that civil law legal systems favour the protection of creditors over equity investors (e.g. Roberts *et al.*, 2002). However, La Porta *et al.* (1998) find no evidence that certain types of investors are favoured by civil law countries. Indeed, they conclude that common law countries favour investors *generally*, regardless of security type (i.e., equity or debt). La Porta *et al.* (1997) show that countries with civil law systems have underdeveloped capital markets as a consequence of deficiencies in legal rules in investor protection. In particular, they find that French civil law countries offer the least investor protection and have the lowest quality of enforcement. Furthermore, they find that these deficiencies lead to low levels of external ownership.

3.2.3 Taxation

The alignment between regulations for taxable profit and financial reporting profit is often cited as a determinant of variation in international financial reporting. In certain countries, tax allowances may only be claimed if they are contained in financial reporting information. Therefore, accounting policies used for computing taxable profits dictate the policies used in preparing financial statements for public disclosure. A close alignment between the two profit measures will also be likely to lead to a reporting of profit which minimises the tax liability, and will thus systematically create conservative measures of income. Furthermore, asset measurements may be affected by accelerated depreciation policies in countries where financial reporting profit is used for computing the tax liability. For example, in France, the depreciation rates and useful asset lives used for financial reporting are typically the same as those used for taxation purposes. Similarly, in Germany, any deductions from taxable income must also be included in the commercial balance sheet (Macharzina and Langer, 2002).

Although the literature often provides examples of countries with a strong or weak alignment between taxable and financial reporting profits, the distinction is often unclear. While civil law countries are usually associated with similar tax and financial reporting rules, there are exceptions. A well-cited example is the US, which in general is characterised by independent financial reporting and taxable profits, yet certain stock valuation methods are permitted by the Internal Revenue Service (IRS) for tax purposes only if they are applied in financial reporting disclosures.

3.2.4 The accounting profession

An adequate supply of professionally qualified accountants is a necessary precursor to the development and application of a comprehensive set of financial reporting regulations and requirements. Therefore, the size of the accountancy profession is also often argued to be a partial determinant of international accounting differences (e.g., Nobes and Parker, 2002; Roberts *et al.*, 2002). However, there are substantial variations and inconsistencies in the size and characteristics of national accounting professions.

Nobes and Parker (2002) attribute a large accounting profession to financing systems dominated by outside equity finance and the associated divorce of ownership and control. Thus, the providers of finance are less informed than in debt-based systems and as such need to be assured that the information conveyed by management is reliable and verified by qualified auditors. This is reflected in the most important accounting professions being located in equity-based countries such as the UK, Canada, the US and Australia.

In addition to the size of the accounting profession, differences in the *influence* of the accounting profession have also been considered a determinant of differences in financial reporting systems. The influence and perception of the profession is clearly linked to the credibility which users afford to the financial statements generated and verified by its members. In common law countries, the profession generally assumes a regulatory role, and in some cases has at its disposal sanctions for non-compliance by companies.[1] However, in civil law countries, accounting regulations are normally set and enforced by the government, although the profession is likely to be consulted and have some input to the process (Roberts *et al.*, 2002).

3.2.5 Consolidation of determinants of international accounting differences

In a recent synthesis of the comparative international accounting literature, Nobes (1998) proposes a 'general model' of international financial reporting differences. He argues that differences in international financial reporting are primarily attributable to differences in the objectives of financial reporting systems. In turn, these objectives are identified by Nobes as the product of (i) the type of financing system and (ii) colonial inheritance. For the type of financing system, Nobes develops a classification based first on the predominant source of finance (i.e., debt versus equity) and second on the influence of insiders (e.g., families and banks) and outsiders (such as private investors).

Two types of financial reporting systems emerge from Nobes' analysis; these are labelled Class A and Class B. Anglo-Saxon accounting systems such as the US, the UK and Australia typify the Class A classification, where accounting practice is not closely aligned with tax rules and where equity-outsider markets predominate. By contrast, Class B systems traditionally have accounting practices closely aligned with tax rules and weak equity markets, but generally, strong insider-credit finance sources. The orientation of these two systems influences both accounting measurement and information disclosure. Equity (specifically, equity-outsider) driven systems are orientated towards providing information to aid investment decisions and providing information for the prediction of future cash flows. Creditor

[1] For example, in the UK, the Financial Reporting Review Panel may apply to the courts to require revision of company accounts.

dominated systems, however, are required to calculate profit for both distribution purposes and taxation purposes. The second primary factor determining the orientation of the financial reporting system identified by Nobes (1998), colonial inheritance, acknowledges that financial reporting systems are often shaped by historical events, rather than by financing traditions.

Nobes (1998) argues that the remaining factors considered by prior researchers into international accounting differences are less useful as determinants of international financial reporting differences, viewing such factors as consequences of the type of financing system and colonial inheritance. For example, the exclusion of taxation as a cause of international accounting differences is attributed to the fact that the disparity between profits for financial reporting and taxation is a consequence of the type of financing system. Specifically, taxable profit figures are vital as a basis for the determination of companies' tax liability in all countries which tax profits. However, the presence of outsiders as providers of finance creates the demand for profit measurement for decision making, which is incongruent with taxable profit.

The numerous factors put forward as explanations for international accounting differences in the literature have, therefore, been distilled over time. From an original list of 17 factors identified, two factors have been pin-pointed as the most significant in the most recent study.

3.2.6 The classification of accounting systems

Attempts to classify accounting systems by identifying common characteristics and historical patterns can be separated into two main approaches: *intrinsic* classifications and *extrinsic* classifications (Roberts, 1995). Intrinsic classifications generally involve the application of data reduction techniques such as factor analysis to classify groups of countries according to their accounting practices.

A good example is Da Costa *et al.* (1978), who used data collected on 38 countries to test the existence of American, British and continental European models of accounting practices. Despite their a priori expectations, Da Costa *et al.* only found empirical support for a two-way classification of US and British models. Furthermore, some inconsistencies emerged from their analysis. The British group followed a pattern attributed to Britain's colonial influence, yet India was classified in the US group. No evidence of a 'continental' set of practices emerged from the data despite Germany, France, Spain, Switzerland and Italy being included in the sample.

Inconsistencies with prior accounting research has led other academic commentators to question the validity of the results of such empirically-driven studies. For example, Nobes (1981; 1983) is critical of the exaggeration of the differences between UK and US accounting and the simultaneous understatement of the variation between Britain and other countries. Specifically, Nobes (1983, p. 3) states that the contention that UK accounting is more similar to accounting in Uruguay and Ethiopia than to US accounting 'is clearly a very inaccurate representation of the real world', despite the statistical authenticity of the result.

In contrast to the intrinsic classifications described above, extrinsic classifications classify countries according to *influential* factors on accounting practices, rather than the practices themselves. Two important studies exemplifying the extrinsic approach are Seidler (1967) and AAA (1977). The former classified accounting systems according to 'spheres of influence' (i.e., British, American and Continental) and the latter in terms of 'zones of influence' (British, Franco – Spanish – Portuguese, German – Dutch, USA and Communist).

Nobes (1983) represents a development of the intrinsic classification studies in that his methodology combined statistical analysis with judgement, based on his experience with the countries involved. Nobes identified two groups of countries based on country scores on issues including the importance of tax rules, the degree of conservatism and the rigidity of the regulations on accounting provisions. The first group (labelled micro-based) comprised Netherlands, UK, Ireland, Australia, New Zealand, Canada and the USA. The second (macro-uniform) group comprised France, Belgium, Spain, Italy, Germany, Japan and Sweden. Within the micro classification, Nobes distinguished between UK and US influenced countries. Macro-uniform countries were also split into tax versus law-based countries. However, Nobes' classification only covered Western developed economies, and inconsistencies appeared between the statistical and judgmental methods. For example, the cluster analysis grouped Australia as being more closely aligned with the USA than the UK, whereas the initial scoring methods implied the opposite.

Berry (1987) provides an extended version of Nobes' (1983) macro/micro classification. Although Berry's classification procedures and criteria are unclear, his classification contains over 3 times as many countries as Nobes (48 versus 14 respectively). Thus, Berry also incorporates 11 communist countries and 9 South American capitalist countries, both within the macro-uniform cluster. Berry also includes 13 British commonwealth countries within the micro 'UK influence' cluster (except for Bermuda, which forms part of the 'US influence' cluster). For the countries included in both Berry's and Nobes' analyses, however, there is overall consistency in the macro/micro classification.

Doupnik and Salter (1993) use cluster analysis to provide empirical support for Nobes' (1983) and Berry's (1987) judgmental classifications.

Doupnik and Salter's analysis is therefore informed by judgement and experience, and tested by more objective statistical processes. Furthermore, their data were collected in the 1990s, and due to their methodology, they avoided the weaknesses of other statistically-based classifications such as Da Costa *et al.* (1978).

The dichotomous clusters generated by Doupnik and Salter's (1993) analysis conform to the macro-uniform and micro groups identified by Nobes and extended by Berry. In particular, there was 100% correct classification of countries in Nobes' (1983) macro/micro groups. Berry's placement of British commonwealth countries (excluding Bermuda) within the UK influence cluster of the micro group also received emphatic empirical support. Furthermore, systematic differences were identified between the two groups in respect of both measurement and disclosure practices. Doupnik and Salter found a greater degree of compliance with International Accounting Standards Committee (IASC) recommended measurement practices and higher levels of disclosure by the micro group, relative to macro-uniform countries. Overall, therefore, countries in the micro group (generally influenced either by the UK or the US) use accounting measurement and disclosure practices more consistent with the needs of equity investors.

While stereotypes abound in the classification of accounting systems, therefore, such stereotypes are not always supported empirically, and may be ill-founded. The important question that arises from this is: what are the consequences of differences in international accounting and financial reporting systems? The next two sections examine the results of research into the effects of these differences on first, reported accounting figures, and second, on stock markets.

3.3 THE EFFECTS OF INTERNATIONAL ACCOUNTING DIVERSITY ON REPORTED FIGURES

There is a wealth of prior research into the effects of international accounting differences on reported accounting results. One widely used method is the conservatism index first developed by Gray (1980). This index entails comparison with some form of benchmark adjusted profit and is given by:

$$1 - \left(\frac{R_A - R_D}{|R_A|} \right)$$

where R_A = adjusted profit (in the case of Gray (1980), profit prepared in accordance with the standardised method developed by the European Federation of Financial Analysts Societies) and R_D = disclosed profit.

Companies with a ratio greater than 1 are considered optimistic, whereas companies with ratios less than 1 are considered relatively conservative.

Gray found that country factors were statistically significant determinants of profit measurement. Specifically, he found that French and German companies are more conservative than UK companies. However, the adjustments made to arrive at the benchmark profit did not include adjustments for important items such as stock valuation and depreciation.[2]

In a more recent study employing the same methodology, Weetman and Gray (1990) use SEC reconciliation data required under Form 20-F to examine differences between UK and US reported profits. They found that the differences between the two regimes are significant, with UK reported profits being systematically less conservative than US profits (up to 25% on average). The adjustments causing these discrepancies mainly related to goodwill (UK profits were higher due to immediate write off to reserves rather than amortisation through the income statement) and deferred taxation.

The introduction of FRS 10 almost certainly means that these differences will now not be so substantial. However, more recently, Pope and Walker (1999) find differences in the timeliness and conservatism of earnings between the UK and the US. They find that earnings before extraordinary items are more conservative for companies reporting under US GAAP than those using UK GAAP. Therefore, these results demonstrate that significant differences in reported figures can exist between the UK and the US – countries generally assumed to share many similar characteristics. For example, both countries' legal systems are common-law based, and the UK and the US both have strong equity markets and accounting professions. Moreover, both countries are also grouped together in many accounting classification studies.

Bandyopadhyay *et al.* (1994) also found that accounting differences in reported profits between regimes which are apparently very similar, can still be significant. They compared reported accounting data prepared under Canadian accounting standards and US GAAP for 96 firms listed on both Canadian and US equity markets, and found that differences are often substantial relative to market capitalisation and reported earnings. For example, 50% of the sample firms experienced total differences in earnings outside a range of positive 0.5% of market capitalisation (i.e., where US GAAP earnings were greater than Canadian GAAP earnings) to negative 1.9% of market capitalisation (US GAAP earnings were lower than Canadian earnings).

[2] Gray (1980, p. 71) conjectures that given the relatively strong links between accounting and taxable profits in France and Germany, these factors are likely to lead to increased conservatism.

In a comparison of civil and code law countries, Ball *et al.* (2000) demonstrate that institutional factors can have a substantial influence on the properties of accounting income. They found that earnings are less volatile in civil law countries due to the pressure for stable income from users of financial information (for example, the government). In contrast to the results of much prior research, Ball *et al.* found that civil law countries were *less* conservative in their incorporation of economic losses into accounting income. However, they distinguish income conservatism from balance sheet conservatism (understating assets and/or overstating liabilities). They argue that their results are attributable to greater demand for timely disclosure of economic losses in common law countries.

3.3.1 Example of US/German GAAP differences: BASF

In order to illustrate how accounting differences manifest themselves at the individual company level, Table 3.2 compares the reported figures for the same company under different accounting principles. The data are taken from SEC Form 20-F for the German chemicals company, BASF A.G., for the year ending 31 December 2003. The income statement and shareholders' equity are presented in accordance with German GAAP; these figures are then reconciled to US GAAP, as required by the SEC for all non-US companies listed on US stock markets.

To the extent that the German GAAP-based income and balance sheet figures are lower for both 2003 and 2002, the figures support the view discussed above that German accounting is generally more conservative than US accounting. Net income under US GAAP is 47% higher than under German GAAP in 2003, and 17% higher in 2003. Moreover, shareholders' equity under US GAAP is 8.5% higher under US GAAP at the end of 2003 and almost 6% higher at the end of 2002. It is likely that these differences are at the lower end of the distribution (and thus underestimate the average German/US GAAP differences) as large multinational companies such as BASF are more likely to choose accounting policies which conform, as much as is permitted in their home countries, to US GAAP (Nobes, 2002).

More detailed examination of Form 20-F revealed that the two principal drivers of the differences in income in 2003 are provisions and goodwill. German accounting rules are relatively permissive regarding the creation of provisions. These may be used to lower income (and often corporation tax liability), but particularly to smooth income through the contribution to provisions during periods of strong performance and the release of such

Table 3.2 Reconciliation of German GAAP and US GAAP for BASF A.G.

	Y/E 31/12/03 (€ millions)	Y/E 31/12/02 (€ millions)
Reconciliation of net income		
Net income as reported in the Consolidated Financial Statements of income under German GAAP	**910.2**	**1,504.4**
Adjustments required to conform with U.S. GAAP:		
Capitalisation of interest	(7.3)	(6.4)
Capitalisation of software developed for internal use	(2.8)	30.5
Accounting for pensions	69.0	71.2
Accounting for provisions	157.6	12.4
Accounting for derivatives at fair value and valuation of long-term foreign currency items at year end rates	(24.8)	(143.9)
Valuation of securities at market values	(6.2)	–
Valuation adjustments relating to companies accounted for under the equity method	62.4	12.9
Reversal of goodwill amortisation and write-offs due to permanent impairment	167.3	211.0
Other adjustments	1.0	(12.9)
Deferred taxes and recognition of tax credit for dividend payments	0.6	48.1
Minority interests	10.7	(10.4)
Net income in accordance with U.S. GAAP	**1,337.7**	**1,716.9**
Reconciliation of shareholders' equity to US GAAP		
Stockholders' equity as reported in the Consolidated Balance Sheet under German GAAP	**15,878.4**	**16,942.2**
Minority interests	(388.1)	(396.3)
Stockholders' equity excluding minority interests	15,490.3	16,545.9
Adjustments required to conform with U.S. GAAP:		
Capitalisation of interest	493.9	542.8
Capitalisation of software developed for internal use	184.1	192.8
Accounting for pensions	982.5	914.0
Accounting for provisions	206.8	49.4
Accounting for derivatives at fair value and valuation of long-term foreign currency items at year end rates	(138.8)	(115.1)
Valuation of securities at market values	89.1	100.6
Valuation adjustments relating to companies accounted for under the equity method	182.0	138.3
Reversal of goodwill amortisation and write-offs due to permanent impairment	337.1	207.4
Other adjustments	43.4	58.5
Deferred taxes and recognition of tax credit for dividend payments	(633.3)	(688.8)
Minority interests	(15.3)	(26.0)
Stockholders' equity in accordance with U.S. GAAP	**17,221.8**	**17,919.8**

provisions during bad years in order to supplement income (Macharzina and Langer, 2002). The use of such discretionary provisions is forbidden under US GAAP and International Accounting Standards. The majority of the € 157.6 million difference for 2003 is attributable to differences in provisions for pre-retirement programs for employees (€ 124.4 million) and provisions for restructuring (€ 23.5 million).

The goodwill reversal of € 167.3 million is due to German GAAP requiring amortisation over its useful life and US GAAP requiring write-offs only in accordance with impairment testing. Thus, BASF had no requirements to write-down goodwill under US GAAP, so the charge in the German accounts is added back to income (and to shareholders' equity). Such differences are not unusual as the amortisation of goodwill is often the principal cause of accounting differences in non-US companies' reconciliations to US GAAP (Weetman and Gray, 1998).

In the case of the shareholders' equity reconciliation for 2003, the two largest items are for pensions (increases equity by € 982.5 million) and deferred taxation (reduces equity by € 633 million. The pensions adjustment is due to prepaid pension assets arising from US/German GAAP differences in valuations of pension obligations and assets which are not recorded on the consolidated balance sheet under German GAAP. The adjustment for deferred taxation is due to US/German GAAP differences in the asset values contained in the consolidated balance sheet for financial reporting and those used for tax purposes. The reconciliation also contains an asset under US GAAP of € 493.9 million for the capitalised value of interest on borrowings for large capital projects; under German GAAP, this expenditure is required to be written off in the year in which it is incurred.

What both academic research and the data in Table 3.2 demonstrate is that international differences between accounting regimes inevitably feed through to substantial differences in bottom-line figures, meaning that international comparisons of financial statements need to be made with caution. Although, at first sight, adjustment of financial statements may appear to resolve such problems, this is not necessarily the case: even after adjusting accounting figures to a common basis, significant differences may exist. In a study of US, Japanese and Korean firms, Choi *et al.* (1983) found substantial differences in financial ratios based on unadjusted (i.e., domestic) figures. However, even *after* restatement to common accounting principles (in this case, US GAAP), differences still existed in the ratios of firms from different countries. These differences are attributable to institutional, cultural, political and tax considerations, and thus do not necessarily reflect variation in financial risk or return characteristics of the companies. McLeay (2002) also argues that international financial analysis needs to take account of wider issues, such as national social structure, due to their impact on reported accounting data.

3.4 THE EFFECTS OF INTERNATIONAL ACCOUNTING DIFFERENCES ON STOCK MARKETS

While prior research clearly indicates that national characteristics have a material effect on reported accounting figures, the findings of research into how accounting differences affect share prices and share returns are contradictory. The most common way to investigate this issue is to measure the level of statistical association between reported figures and share prices and returns in regression analysis. If the accounting figures are significantly associated with stock market variables, they are considered 'value relevant'.

It is currently the subject of a vigorous debate in the academic literature, however, whether this measure is appropriate for assessing accounting standards. Holthausen and Watts (2001) argue, *inter alia*, that the value relevance literature does not capture what standard setters regard as the most important characteristics of an accounting system; moreover, they challenge the assumptions made by this research about market values being an appropriate benchmark against which accounting numbers should be compared. However, Barth *et al.* (2001) challenge many of these points. Nevertheless, it is currently the primary way to operationalise research into how relevant and reliable accounting data are to investors in equity valuation.

In a comparison of the value relevance of German and US accounting measures, Harris *et al.* (1994) hypothesised that German accounting measures have low explanatory power for share prices/returns relative to US measures. They tested this hypothesis using the following regression model:

$$\frac{P_{jt} + d_{jt} - P_{jt-1}}{P_{jt-1}} = \alpha_{0t} + \alpha_{1t}\frac{X_{jt} - X_{jt-1}}{P_{jt-1}} + \alpha_{2t}\frac{X_{jt}}{P_{jt-1}} + \varepsilon_{jt} \tag{3.1}$$

where j and t are subscripts for firm j and time t, P is share price, d is dividend per share, X = accounting earnings per share and ε is the regression error term. Harris *et al.* hypothesised that the regression coefficients for earnings and changes in earnings (i.e., α_1 and α_2) will be zero if these variables are not value relevant, i.e., if accounting data are used by investors when valuing German companies. The explanatory power (i.e., coefficient of determination or R^2) of accounting numbers for share prices and returns will therefore also be affected. Despite these expectations,

Harris *et al.* found a significant association between German accounting data and share prices. Interestingly, although the earnings coefficient (α_2) was significantly larger for German earnings (consistent with more conservative accounting), the strength of association between earnings and returns in Germany was comparable to that in the United States. Adjustments made to German accounting measures by German financial analysts (DVFA) modestly increased the explanatory power of earnings for returns.

In a similar study, Joos and Lang (1994) provided evidence that measurement practices in Germany are more conservative than those in the UK and France. Despite expectations of a stronger relationship between accounting data and share prices in the UK relative to France and Germany, they found that the value relevance of UK accounting data is comparable to the value relevance of French and German accounting data.

More recently, however, Ali and Hwang (2000) found that externally reported accounting data are less value relevant in countries where bank-oriented financial systems dominate, such as in Germany. As banks have direct access to management, Ali and Hwang argue that the demand for financial information is lower in bank-orientated systems than in stock market oriented systems. They also found that the value relevance of financial reports is lower for countries which have no private sector standard setting, where accounting rules are closely aligned with tax rules, and where expenditure on audit services is low.

Overall, the lack of consensus of the research into the impact of international accounting differences on share prices suggests that findings are sensitive to the companies, time period or statistical models used. In general, however, in countries where equity is not the primary source of finance, reported results appear to be more conservative. Furthermore, the most recent research indicates that accounting information in these countries is less relevant for company valuation. Regulatory efforts are currently being devoted to the erosion of international accounting differences. The following section discusses the background to harmonisation and the institutions involved, with particular attention paid to the International Accounting Standards Board (IASB).

3.5 THE INTERNATIONAL HARMONISATION OF ACCOUNTING

The preceding literature shows that international accounting differences are significant and may be responsible for variation in the relevance of accounting information for valuing companies. Since 1904, private and public sector regulatory bodies have been attempting to reduce these international accounting differences via a process of harmonisation (Chandler, 1992). Various organisations are contributing to these efforts. The United Nations has established an intergovernmental working group which links representatives from developed and developing economies to discuss financial reporting issues and the Organization for Economic Cooperation and Development (OECD) has also set up a working group on accounting standards which has addressed certain accounting issues and issued guidelines for multinational enterprises. However, neither of the above bodies actually issues accounting standards and, to date, the main regulatory efforts in Europe have originated from the IASB and the European Union (EU).

It should be noted that harmonisation is not driven entirely by regulation. As noted earlier, outside the EU, non-US firms seeking access to US securities markets must reconcile their accounts to US GAAP if differences between domestic and US reported figures are material. The relative attractiveness of US equity markets means that many companies are willing to bear the costs of reconciliation and prepare their financial statements according to US GAAP. Market forces, combined with the enforcement of regulations by the SEC, are therefore also narrowing international accounting practices.

The IASB now represents the most potent force in the international accounting standard-setting arena. This London-based organisation can be traced back to an agreement between accounting bodies from nine countries in 1973, following proposals in a meeting of the Accountant International Study Group (AISG) in Sydney the previous year (Chandler, 1992). Since its formation, the IASB has grown to represent the interests of around 90 different countries.

The IASB's mission is to develop 'a single set of high quality, understandable and enforceable global accounting standards that require transparent and comparable information in general purpose financial statements' (IASB web-site – www.iasb.org). Its inception has been attributed to the demand for comparable accounting information, which in turn has arisen from the internationalisation of capital markets (Thorell and Whittington, 1994). Between its formation in 1973 and its demise in 2001, the predecessor of the IASB (the International Accounting Standards Committee – the IASC) issued 41 standards on a broad range of accounting issues. The IASC was then superseded by the IASB in June 2001.

The European Union (via the European Commission) has also been actively pursuing harmonisation, and has issued numerous Directives relevant to accounting. The most influential Directives in the context of harmonisation are the Fourth and Seventh. Since November 1995, however, the IASB and the EU have co-operated with a view to introducing IAS across Europe by 2005. Some have seen this as an attempt to head-off the SEC becoming the *de facto* standard-setter for Europe's largest companies (Flower, 1997).

To perceive the IASC purely as a product of demand from capital markets for comparable accounting information is, however, to ignore its political history. Despite their recent alignment of interests, the relationship between the IASC and the EU has historically been somewhat antagonistic. In this context, the IASC has been viewed as a vehicle through which other organisations have sought to pursue their own political agendas. In particular, Hopwood (1994) argues that the IASC was used by the UK audit industry as a means of modifying the Fourth Directive so that the concept of 'true and fair view', and its emphasis on auditor judgement, was maintained. Hopwood (1994, p. 244) also attributes the recent prominence of the IASC to attempts by the SEC, through the International Organization of Securities Commissions (IOSCO), to 're-energize the slumbering IASC into constructing an international basis for accounting disclosures that would be acceptable to the USA and, possibly because of its international rather than American origins, more acceptable to the wider community'. Hopwood is not the only academic commentator to recognise the pragmatic and political complexities involved in the harmonisation process. Ball (1995) contends that one set of global accounting rules would be inflexible and inevitably politically driven. Ball argues that harmonisation is not necessarily desirable because national accounting systems have evolved to reflect country-specific characteristics, such as user needs and financial reporting objectives.

Even if these barriers are overcome, harmonisation is not without costs. Barth *et al.* (1999) suggest that harmonisation can have detrimental effects on security markets, and recommend that caution should be exercised by regulators and standard-setters in their harmonisation efforts. In a theoretical mathematical model of global trading and international accounting differences, they show that under certain conditions, positive characteristics of capital market performance (i.e., price informativeness and liquidity) can be negatively affected by harmonisation.

Meanwhile, Goeltz (1991) argues that the 'explosive' growth in international securities transactions in recent years constitutes evidence that investors are able to make decisions despite international accounting differences. He asserts that rational investors are able to see through international accounting differences to the real economic performance of the firm as effective use of financial data can overcome incomparability. In particular, Goeltz argues that accounts prepared on the basis of its domestic standards are likely to be sufficient and that there is no demonstrated need for global accounting standards in order to fuel the growth of strong international capital markets. Goeltz points to the success of non-US companies issuing equity under the SEC Rule 144A as evidence of the insignificance of accounting differences. This rule provides exemption from reconciliation requirements for securities issued (i.e. placed) only to authorised financial institutions. Between its introduction in 1990 and 1996, Rule 144A attracted 197 firms from 35 countries to issue finance (Foerster and Karolyi, 2000) and the absence of SEC reconciliation requirements does not appear to have deterred investors from using this facility.

3.5.1 The rationale for international accounting harmonisation

While multinational corporations and international accounting and auditing firms have been found to support harmonisation because they perceive it will reduce reporting costs of listing on foreign equity markets, the principal rationale for international accounting harmonisation is that increased comparability of financial statements is necessary to aid investors' decision making. For example, Cairns (1994, p. 343) states:

> International capital markets demand financial statements that can be really understood and compared irrespective of country of origin of the companies concerned. Investors and their advisers, the financial analysts, want financial statements that are comparable from country to country so that they can compare the financial statements of enterprises in New York, London, Tokyo, Toronto, Copenhagen, Frankfurt, Paris, Rome and so on.

Much academic research on international harmonisation alludes to similar reasons for harmonisation, citing the demand from investors for increased comparability as the main justification (e.g., Samuels and Piper, 1985; Chandler, 1992; Thorrell and Whittington, 1994; Schweikart *et al.*, 1996). International accounting differences are often perceived as barriers to investment, and investors and analysts are generally assumed to offer unqualified support for the harmonisation process.

Examination of the academic literature reveals that such a straightforward and disinterested rationale is not universally accepted. For example, Taylor (1987) argues that the IASC is only supported by self-interested Anglo-American professions with highly developed capital markets. Taylor challenges the most popular rationales for the IASC and claims that the demand for international accounting standards originates from Anglo-American professions and firms. This is so these firms can maintain self-regulation in countries where the profession is not self-regulated, and to increase complexity of accounting practices by enforcing Anglo-American standards. Furthermore, Taylor argues that Anglo-American accounting firms promote international accounting standards to reduce world-wide training costs.

The contention that investors and analysts offer unqualified support for international accounting harmonisation has itself also been challenged. While there are examples of support for harmonisation from the investment community in the academic literature (e.g., Roach, 1996), such cases are few and far between. The only study to examine this issue systematically is Marton (1998). He found that analysts are generally supportive of harmonisation, although this was based on a relatively small sample of 15 analysts.[3] Consequently, questions have been raised about the demand for comparable accounting information from analysts and investors so commonly referred to in the literature. Hopwood (1994) argues that users of accounting information such as institutional investors are represented rhetorically rather than physically in the international accounting policy arena, pointing out that the international financial and investment communities have been virtually silent in over 20 years of international accounting deliberations.

3.5.2 Analysts' and investors' participation in international accounting standard setting

Consistent with Hopwood's arguments, research into the involvement in the international accounting standard setting process reveals a surprising lack of participation by the investment community – a finding somewhat incongruous with their supposed urgent needs for comparable information. Kenny and Larson (1995), for example, found that of 745 comment letters to exposure drafts, only 26 (3.5%) were from analysts. Even if it is recognised that analysts and investors may not necessarily be highly involved in the detail of technical accounting standard setting, the fact that one of the exposure drafts (ED 32) related specifically to comparability of financial reporting is evidence of low interest from the investment community. Larson (1997) also found that companies rather than users are more active in the international accounting standards lobbying process.

This inconsistency between references to the needs of capital market users for comparable information and the apparent lack of involvement in the harmonisation process has led to calls for research into this issue. In particular, Hopwood (1994, p. 250) states that 'at present we have all too minimal an understanding of transnational information processing and use. It would be useful if some studies of the actual functioning of transnational accounting were available to confront the mere assumptions that currently underlie much policy-making in the arena.'

[3] Marton's study is discussed further in Chapter 5.

It is therefore far from universally accepted that harmonisation is necessarily a worthwhile goal, let alone whether it is a goal desired by capital market participants. Although the political process has been characterised by a lack of participation by users of accounting information such as analysts and institutional investors, this does not necessarily mean that they have no interest in international accounting harmonisation. It may be the case that the financial community perceives the costs of participation or lobbying to be prohibitive relative to the benefits. In a similar context, Sutton (1984) examined participation in the domestic standard setting process in the US and UK. Sutton provided a framework for analysing the lobbying decision, where individuals lobby when perceived benefits exceed the costs, expressing the benefits of lobbying as a product of two variables: first, the difference in utility following a desirable outcome in the election/decision; and second, the probability that the lobbyist will affect the outcome. He found that producers of financial statements are more likely to engage in lobbying activities than users of financial statements, and like the international standard setting arena, users were poorly represented in the UK lobbying process.

3.6 SUMMARY

The literature discussed in this chapter has shown that international accounting differences are significant and are attributable to factors such as international variation in legal and financial environments. The most recent research into the causes of these differences suggests that the primary determinant of national accounting systems is the nature of the dominant providers of finance, i.e., countries where companies are primarily financed by debt will have different (and possibly lower) levels of disclosure. In addition to having a marked impact upon reported accounting figures, international accounting differences may also cause variation in the relevance of accounting information to stock market users, although the research has yet to reach a clear consensus on this issue.

This chapter has also described the substantial regulatory efforts, primarily by the International Accounting Standards Board, to reduce variations in international accounting via the harmonisation process. The rationale for harmonisation (that the financial community involved in transnational decisions requires comparable information) was examined critically. In particular, prior research demonstrates a relative lack of involvement of institutional investors and investment analysts in the harmonisation process. However, there has been a distinct lack of research into how the financial community views the harmonisation process. The empirical study presented later in the book seeks to address this issue.

3.7 REFERENCES

AAA (1977). 'Report of the American Accounting Association Committee on International Accounting Operations and Education.' *The Accounting Review*, Supplement, 67–119.

Ali, A. and Hwang, L. (2000). 'Country-specific factors related to financial reporting and the value relevance of accounting data.' *Journal of Accounting Research*, **38** (1), 1–21.

Ball, R. (1995). 'Making accounting more international: why, how and how far will it go?' *Journal of Applied Corporate Finance*, **8** (3), 19–29.

Ball, R., Kothari, S.P. and Robin, A. (2000). 'The effect of international institutional factors on properties of accounting earnings.' *Journal of Accounting and Economics*, **29**, 1–51.

Bandyopadhyay, S.P., Hanna, J.D. and Richardson, G. (1994). 'Capital market effects of US–Canada GAAP differences.' *Journal of Accounting Research*, **32** (2), 262–277.

Barth, M., Clinch, G. and Shibano, T. (1999). 'International accounting harmonisation and global equity markets.' *Journal of Accounting and Economics*, **26**, 201–235.

Barth, M.E., Beaver, W.H. and Landsman, W.R. (2001). 'The relevance of the value-relevance literature for financial accounting standard setting: another view.' *Journal of Accounting and Economics*, **31**, 77–104.

Berry, I. (1987). 'The need to classify worldwide practices.' *Accountancy*, **October**, 90–91.

Cairns, D. (1994). 'What is the future of mutual recognition of financial statements and is comparability really necessary?' *The European Accounting Review*, **3**, 343–352.

Chandler, R. (1992). 'The international harmonisation of accounting: in search of influence.' *International Journal of Accounting*, **27**, 222–233.

Choi, F.D.S., Hino, H. and Min, S., Kee. (1983). 'Analyzing foreign financial statements: the use and misuse of international ratio analysis.' *Journal of International Business Studies*, **Spring-Summer**, 113–131.

Choi, F.D.S., Frost, C.A. and Meek, G.K. (1999). *International Accounting*. 3rd edn. Prentice-Hall, New Jersey.

Da Costa, R.C., Bourgeois, J.C. and Lawson, W.M. (1978). 'A classification of international financial accounting practices.' *International Journal of Accounting*, **Spring**, 73–86.

David, R. and Brierley, J.E.C. (1985). *Major Legal Systems in the World Today*, 3rd edn, Stevens and Sons, London.

Doupnik, T.S. and Salter, S.B. (1993). 'An empirical test of a judgmental international classification of financial reporting practices.' *Journal of International Business Studies*, **24** (1), 41–60.

Flower, J. (1997). 'The future shape of harmonisation: the EU versus the IASC versus the SEC.' *The European Accounting Review*, **6** (2), 281–303.

Foerster, S.R. and Karolyi, G.A. (2000). 'The long run performance of global equity offerings.' *Journal of Financial and Quantitative Analysis*, **35** (4), 499–528.

Goeltz, R.K. (1991). 'International accounting harmonisation: the impossible (and unnecessary?) dream.' *Accounting Horizons*, **March**, 85–88.

Gray, S.J. (1980). 'The impact of international accounting differences from a security-analysis perspective: some European evidence.' *Journal of Accounting Research*, **18** (1), 64–76.

Gray, S.J. (1988). 'Towards a theory of cultural influence on the development of accounting systems internationally.' *Abacus*, **24** (1), 1–15.

Harris, T.S., Lang, M. and Moller, H.P. (1994). 'The value relevance of German accounting measures: an empirical analysis.' *Journal of Accounting Research*, **32** (2), 187–209.

Holthausen, R.W. and Watts, R.L. (2001). 'The relevance of the value-relevance literature for financial accounting standard setting.' *Journal of Accounting and Economics*, **31**, 3–75.

Hopwood, A.G. (1994). 'Some reflections On "The Harmonization of Accounting Within the EU".' *The European Accounting Review*, **3** (2), 241–253.

Joos, P. and Lang, M. (1994). 'The effects of accounting diversity: evidence from the European Union.' *Journal of Accounting Research*, **32**, Supplement, 141–168.

Kenny, S.Y. and Larson, R.K. (1995). 'The development of international accounting standards: an analysis of constituent participation in standards setting.' *International Journal of Accounting*, **30**, 283–301.

La Porta, R. Lopez-De-Silanes, F., Shleifer, A. and Vishny, R.W. (1997). 'Legal determinants of external finance.' *Journal of Finance*, **52** (3), 1131–1150.

La Porta, R., Lopez-De-Silanes, F. and Shleifer, A. (1998). 'Law and finance.' *Journal of Political Economy*, **106** (6), 1113–1155

Larson, R.K. (1997). 'Corporate lobbying of the International Accounting Standards Committee.' *Journal of International Financial Management and Accounting*, **8** (3), 175–203.

Macharzina, K. and Langer, K. (2002) 'Financial reporting in Germany.' In Nobes, C.W. and Parker, R.H. *Comparative International Accounting*, 7th edn, Pearson Education, Harlow.

Marton, J. (1998). *Accounting and Stock Markets: A Study of Swedish Accounting for International Investors and Analysts*, BAS, Gothenburg University, Sweden.

McLeay, S.J. (2002). 'International financial analysis.' In Nobes, C.W. and Parker, R.H. *Comparative International Accounting*, 7th edn, Pearson Education, Harlow.

Nobes, C.W. (1981). 'An empirical analysis of international accounting principles: a comment.' *Journal of Accounting Research*, **19** (1), 268–270.

Nobes, C.W. (1983). 'A judgemental international classification of financial reporting practices.' *Journal of Business Finance and Accounting*, **10** (1), 1–19.

Nobes, C.W. (1998). 'Towards a general model of the reasons for international differences in financial reporting.' *ABACUS*, **34** (2), 162–187.

Nobes, C.W. (2002). 'Some major international differences in financial reporting.' In Nobes, C.W. and Parker, R.H. *Comparative International Accounting*, 7th edn, Pearson Education, Harlow.

Nobes, C.W. and Parker, R. (2002). *Comparative International Accounting*, 7th edn. Prentice Hall, London.

Pope, P.F. and Walker, M. (1999). 'International differences in the timeliness, conservatism and classification of earnings.' *Journal of Accounting Research*, **37**, 53–87.

Roach, N. (1996). 'Global accounting standards: an investor's view.' *Journal of International Financial Management and Accounting*, **7** (1), 74–81.

Roberts, A. (1995). 'The very idea of classification in international accounting.' *Accounting, Organizations and Society*, **20** (7/8), 639–664.

Roberts, C., Weetman, P. and Gordon, P. (2002). *International Financial Accounting: A Comparative Approach*, 2nd edn, FT Prentice-Hall, London.

Samuels, J.M. and Piper, A.G. (1985). *International Accounting: A Survey*, Croom Helm, London.

Schweikart, J.A., Gray, S.J. and Salter, S.B. (1996). 'An interview with Sir Bryan Carsberg, Secretary-General of the International Accounting Standards Committee.' *Accounting Horizons*, **10** (1), 110–117.

Seidler, L.J. (1967). 'International accounting – the ultimate theory course.' *The Accounting Review*, **October**, 775–81.

Sutton, T. (1984). 'Lobbying of accounting standards setting bodies in the UK and the USA: a Downsian analysis.' *Accounting, Organizations and Society*, **9** (1), 81–95.

Taylor, S.L. (1987). 'International accounting standards: an alternative rationale.' *Abacus*, **23** (2), 157–171.

Thorell, P. and Whittington, G. (1994). 'The harmonization of accounting within the EU: problems, perspectives and strategies.' *The European Accounting Review*, **3** (2), 215–239.

Weetman, P. and Gray, S.J. (1990). 'International financial analysis and comparative corporate performance: the impact of UK versus US accounting principles on earnings.' *Journal of International Financial Management and Accounting*, **2** (2), 111–130.

Weetman, P. and Gray, S.J. (1998). 'Profit measurement and UK accounting standards: a case of increasing disharmony in relation to US GAAP and IASs.' *Accounting and Business Research*, **28** (3), 189–208.

4
Equity Analysis Techniques: Theory and Evidence

4.1 INTRODUCTION

Theoretically, equities are valued according to the dividend discount model, which expresses share price as a function of the present value of expected future dividends. In practice, however, fund managers and analysts have been found to use a range of equity analysis methods, many of which involve reliance on information other than dividends.

This chapter reviews the prior research into the equity analysis techniques used by analysts and fund managers. It evaluates the various techniques available and examines the research into how widely each technique is used. It shows that fundamental analysis is by far the most commonly used technique in the analysis of domestic equities. Technical analysis and theoretical techniques such as beta analysis typically play a subsidiary role. This research on the usefulness of the various appraisal techniques is then discussed in light of the theory and evidence on stock market efficiency.

4.2 THE THEORY OF EQUITY VALUATION

In theory, the value of any financial asset is expressed as a function of its expected future cash flows, discounted at an appropriate rate. In the case of ordinary shares, cash flows arise in the form of expected dividends and the expected selling price at the end of the period (e.g., Blake, 2000). Formally, the price of a share at time t is given by:

$$P_t = \sum_{\tau=1}^{T} \frac{E_t[d_{t+\tau}]}{(1+k)^{\tau}} + \frac{E_t[P_T]}{(1+k)^{T}} \qquad (4.1)$$

where P_t is the share price at time t, E_t is the expectations operator based on the information set at time t, d_t represents dividends paid at the end of period t and k is the shareholders' required rate of return (i.e., the company's cost of capital), which is contingent on the riskiness of the firm. The second term in this equation (the terminal value or proceeds from sale) becomes zero as $T \to \infty$, leaving the dividend discount model:

$$P_t = \sum_{\tau=1}^{\infty} \frac{E_t[d_{t+\tau}]}{(1+k)^{\tau}} \tag{4.2}$$

A distinguishing feature of equities is that unlike fixed income securities, such as bonds, equities are valued according to *expected* cash flows, as shareholders are residual claimants, i.e., their returns are received after all other obligations (e.g., debt payments, taxation) have been met by the firm. In contrast to the valuation of a bond, where coupon payments are specified and known (at least in nominal terms) at the outset, cash flows arising as a result of ownership of ordinary shares have to be estimated using the information available at time t.[1]

Despite its apparent simplicity, the dividend discount model is deceptively difficult to apply in practice. The strict form of the model requires a forecast of cash flows into the infinite future. Clearly, however, forecasting dividends over long periods of time can be difficult, particularly in the absence of a historical record of dividend payments. The same applies to the discount rate, which, like cash flows, is likely to vary through time and will therefore require estimation.

There are also theoretical challenges to the dividend discount model. According to Miller and Modigliani (1961), it is not possible to influence the value of a company through manipulation of dividend policy. A firm paying no dividend may be performing well (for instance, Microsoft was incorporated in 1981, yet did not pay its first dividend until 2003), while a firm paying a large dividend may be performing poorly. Penman (1992, p. 467) refers to this as the 'dividend conundrum': 'price is based on future dividends, but observed dividends do not tell us anything about price'.

Given these limitations, it is unsurprising that in a practical context, research clearly demonstrates that investors and analysts use a range of analysis techniques in addition to, and apart from, the dividend discount model. The next section briefly describes and evaluates these various techniques.

[1] The comparison of shares and bonds is useful both because of the similarities and the differences between the two types of asset. Indeed, equities have historically been viewed as variants of bonds. For example, many companies in the late 19th century were expected to have a finite life; legislation determined that utilities were only to exist as public companies for 21 years, after which they were to be saleable to the government (Rutterford, 2004).

4.3 EQUITY ANALYSIS TECHNIQUES USED BY ANALYSTS AND FUND MANAGERS

4.3.1 Fundamental analysis

The most prevalent analysis technique used in domestic equity appraisal is fundamental analysis. Definitions of fundamental analysis in academic studies and text books are almost entirely teleological; that is, fundamental analysis is defined by what it *does* or what it involves, rather than what it *is*. Moreover, there is no real consensus on what constitute 'fundamentals'. Most descriptions are consistent in stating that fundamental analysis involves detailed analysis of firm-specific factors such as accounting information, dividend policy and quality of management. They also typically state that this analysis is conducted in the context of the industry and macroeconomy in which companies operate. Bauman (1996, p. 1) provides a useful and succinct description when he states that 'fundamental analysis involves inferring the value of a business firm's equity without reference to the prices at which the firm's securities trade in the capital markets.

Unlike the pure discounted dividend (cash flow) approach, fundamental analysis relies on a variety of sources of information, such as financial statements, company management, and industry and macroeconomic data. In fundamental analysis, financial statement information actually determines company value; the discounted cash flow approach, on the other hand, views accounting data as mere signals of future dividend payments (Bauman, 1996). However, in common with the dividend discount model, a key characteristic of fundamental analysis is that its ultimate purpose is to arrive at an intrinsic value for the share (or for the company), through the estimation of future economic benefits, discounted at an appropriate level to take account of timing and risk.

Accounting research is increasingly providing a theoretical justification for fundamental analysis by recognising that firm value is a function of accounting book value and expected future earnings, after deduction of a charge for capital (e.g., Peasnell, 1982; Ohlson, 1995).[2] This research is displacing dividends and cash flow as the important valuation attributes with earnings and book value. Payments of dividends are predicted to reduce the value of the firm as they reduce future earnings generation capabilities (Lundholm, 1995). Moreover, the application of fundamental analysis to firm valuation is now perceived as more theoretically appealing than discounted cash flow analysis (Penman, 1992).

[2] Theoretical models of equity analysis based on accounting profits are discussed in more depth in Chapter 5.

4.3.1.1 Research into the use of fundamental analysis by investors and analysts

An examination of the research on the techniques used by institutional investors reveals clearly that fundamental analysis is the most useful and most widely used technique. This result persists over time, across countries and across research methodologies, including questionnaire surveys and various experimental approaches. The study of Arnold and Moizer (1984) is exemplary. Their research involved a questionnaire survey of UK fund managers and investment analysts. Fundamental analysis was widely regarded as the most useful method of investment appraisal, and was used almost always by 76% of analysts. Within the fundamental approach, Arnold and Moizer found that the P/E ratio was a factor frequently considered by analysts and fund managers. Over 80% of respondents attempted to predict a company's P/E ratio, based on prior and predicted earnings.

Interestingly, Arnold and Moizer found a range of approaches to investment appraisal, from 'analytical' to 'artistic', thus acknowledging the diversity in fundamental analysis. The analytical approach was the most popular, and typically involved a systematic analysis of the previous ten years' income statements, including disaggregation of the company's activities. This analysis was conducted to estimate future earnings. By contrast, the 'artistic' approach involved a summary of the annual report, but no systematic forecasting of earnings was conducted.

Moizer and Arnold (1984) found differences between fund managers' and analysts' approaches to investment analysis. Analysts followed fewer companies and were more specialised than fund managers. However, despite these differences, both analysts and fund managers considered fundamental analysis to be the most useful appraisal technique. In a related comparative study, Arnold *et al.* (1984) contrasted the techniques used by analysts in the UK and the US. They found that although fundamental analysis was preferred by analysts in both countries, US analysts rated it as significantly more useful than their UK counterparts. Fundamental analysis was also the most widely used appraisal technique by US analysts and fund managers in a study by Carter and Van Auken (1990).

Research shows that the use of fundamental analysis has persisted over time. In a study of appraisal methods used post 'Big Bang' on the London Stock Exchange, Pike *et al.* (1993) found that the P/E ratio and price to cash flow (P/CF) ratio (as central components of fundamental analysis) were perceived as the most useful techniques. Pike *et al.* (1993) concluded that the usefulness of the appraisal methods changed little in the decade between their study and the research of Arnold and Moizer (1984) despite the significant institutional changes that took place on the London Stock Exchange during this period.

The prevalence of fundamental analysis is not confined to the UK, or indeed to Anglo-Saxon countries. For instance, Vergoossen (1993) found that over 90% of analysts and fund managers use fundamental analysis in the Netherlands. The next most widely-used technique was ratio analysis (i.e., a component of fundamental analysis) which was used by 45% of analysts and fund managers. Meanwhile, Olbert (1994) found that fundamental analysis was by far the most dominant appraisal method in the Swedish market as it was used by 91.2% of analysts. In a survey of investment management and appraisal methods in Hong Kong, Wong and Cheung (1999) confirmed that fundamental analysis remains the predominant technique. They also found that the use of fundamental analysis was positively related to the seniority and experience of analysts and the size of the brokerage house or fund management firm.

Although the price/earnings (P/E) ratio is central to fundamental analysis, recent research by Barker (1999a) shows that the extent of P/E use is contingent upon industrial classification. In a study involving both survey and market based data, Barker found that the P/E ratio is used by analysts of companies in the services, industrial and consumer goods sectors. However, for financial companies and utilities, the dividend yield ratio dominates – a finding partially attributed to the predictability of dividends from companies in these sectors.

Examination of the findings of experimental and behavioural studies also reveals that analysts use techniques consistent with the fundamental approach found in questionnaire surveys. In an experiment involving US analysts, Biggs (1984) found that when provided with financial statements, analysts used two types of search strategies. The first was historical, which relied on past data and trends, and the second was predictive, which involved developing measures of earnings per share (EPS) and predicting what this will be in 3 to 5 years time. Interestingly, the majority of analysts (81%) used highly-structured search patterns and calculated a set of ratios and trends for all companies before they analysed any of the ratios, consistent with the 'analytical approach' identified by Arnold and Moizer (1984).

Bouwman *et al.* (1987) split the investment decision into two separate stages and investigated the relevance of accounting information in each of these stages. The first stage involves using information to discriminate between companies to be accepted and those to be rejected; the second stage involves estimating the potential for the company to generate future earnings. Bouwman *et al.* found that the first stage involved the use of comparable information for screening companies, whereas the second stage involved more qualitative information and segmental analyses.

In an innovative study of US analysts, Hunton and McEwen (1997) examined various dimensions of the investment decision by tracking on a Visual Display Unit (VDU) the information items consulted by analysts when evaluating company performance. Interestingly, they found that the provision of underwriting services positively and significantly increased analysts' quarterly and annual forecast errors, where the bias was positive (consistent with the discussion in Chapter 2 on analysts' incentives). Furthermore, Hunton and McEwen found that analysts who used directive search strategies (i.e., where *specific* items were identified and selected from an information set) were more accurate than analysts who used sequential strategies (i.e., where analysts selected the next item on a list), even after controlling for analysts' experience.

In sum, therefore, empirical research clearly demonstrates that fundamental analysis is the principal technique in domestic equity analysis. This result has persisted over time, across different countries and between different professional groups, i.e., analysts and fund managers.

4.3.2 Technical analysis

In many ways, technical analysis can be best described as the antithesis of fundamental analysis. For example, while fundamental analysis represents an eclectic approach to equity appraisal, technical analysis relies solely on share price data as its input and usually involves analysing individual share prices relative to market averages such as sector or market indices. Furthermore, while fundamental analysis seeks to establish an intrinsic value for a share, technical analysis has no such aim. Technical analysts see the price of a share as being determined purely by prevailing stock market conditions, i.e., by supply and demand, rather than by individual company fundamentals such as earnings and book values. As noted by Edwards *et al.* (2001, p. 4), therefore, technical analysis 'refers to *the study of the action of the market itself* as opposed to the study of the goods in which the market deals' (emphasis in the original).

Technical analysis essentially involves the analysis of past share price movements in order to identify patterns or trends to predict future share prices. Although technical analysts often acknowledge that fundamentals affect the price of shares, they posit that many other factors also have an influence. In particular, technical analysis is based on the assumption that share prices and their movements reflect investors' attitudes to political and psychological factors, and the available economic resources at any particular time (e.g., Blake, 2000). Technical analysts therefore operate trading rules or seek to predict future share price movements based on past price patterns or trading volume data. Trends may be sought in the untransformed prices, or in scaled or transformed data (e.g., logarithms or the square root of prices). Common techniques include price pattern identification, momentum investing and moving average analysis.

Critics of technical analysis point out that, to a degree at least, patterns in share price movements are self-fulfilling. That is, if enough market participants are seeking to identify particular trends, then they are likely to buy and sell shares in such a way so as to reinforce the patterns they are looking for (Firth, 1977). For example, a well known pattern in technical analysis is the 'head and shoulders' pattern. Any rational investor following a technical strategy who identifies what looks like a head and shoulders pattern is likely to buy where the pattern predicts the price will rise, and sell where it predicts the price to fall. But by taking these actions, the investor is actually contributing to the creation of the pattern.

4.3.2.1 Empirical research on the use of technical analysis

Prior research shows that technical analysis is far less widely used than fundamental analysis. Arnold and Moizer (1984) found that technical analysis is ranked 'a poor second' to fundamental analysis by UK fund managers and analysts. This result is consistent with the findings from studies of analysts and fund managers in the US (Arnold *et al.*, 1984), the Netherlands (Vergoossen, 1993) and Hong Kong (Wong and Cheung, 1999).

However, Olbert (1994), in his study of Swedish analysts, suggests that technical analysis is dependent upon the depth of trading on the market involved. He attributes the lack of importance attached to technical analysis by Swedish analysts to the thinly-traded nature of the Swedish stock market. In contrast to Olbert's arguments, Pike *et al.* (1993) find that German analysts use technical analysis more than their British counterparts; this finding is linked to the higher predictability of equity prices (i.e., lower pricing efficiency) on the German market compared to the London market.

4.3.3 Beta analysis

Beta analysis represents a more theoretical approach to equity analysis and involves analysing the relationship between changes in the price of a particular company's share and changes in the value of the market as a whole. Specifically, company betas (β) are a measure of the covariance between particular shares and the market portfolio, and are defined as:

$$\beta_i = \frac{\rho_{im}\sigma_i}{\sigma_m} \tag{4.3}$$

where ρ_{im} is the correlation coefficient between the return on security i and the market m, and σ_i and σ_m are the standard deviation on security i and the market m, respectively. Beta is thus a measure of a security's risk (variability) relative to the market. In order to estimate a company beta, share returns are regressed on the returns of a market average, typically some form of index. Shares with betas in excess of one are classed as 'aggressive' since their returns vary more than the market portfolio, while shares with betas below one are referred to as 'defensive' as their returns are less volatile than the market.

Difficulties in estimating company betas make beta analysis difficult to use in practice. As company betas are weighted averages of the company's individual investment projects and are necessarily based on past data, any changes in company operations strictly require changes in beta. Furthermore, as betas are sensitive to the market index used to proxy the market portfolio, different measures can be obtained for different indices (Foley 1991). Theoretically speaking, and as argued by Roll (1977), any stock market index is ultimately inadequate as the market portfolio contains all asset classes and is therefore impossible to measure.

4.3.3.1 Surveys of the usefulness of beta analysis and discounted cash flow

Despite their academic appeal, more theoretical approaches to equity analysis, such as discounted cash flow (DCF) and beta analysis, are generally regarded as less important than fundamental analysis and technical analysis in domestic equity analysis. Arnold and Moizer (1984) found that beta analysis was only considered 'extremely useful' or 'very useful' by 5% of respondents.

Findings on reliance on the discounted cash flow approach are similar to those from research into the use of beta analysis. In an interview preceding Arnold and Moizer's questionnaire survey, one analyst commented upon the mathematical appeal of the DCF method, but acknowledged its excess precision, which was deemed to conflict with the 'inexact nature' of equity investment. More recently, Barker (1999b) found DCF analysis and the dividend discount model to be of little practical importance to either fund managers or analysts. Each of these techniques was, on average, viewed as hardly important. This was attributed to the practical difficulties in obtaining reliable longer-term information, thus limiting valuation to short-term horizons. Studies of analysts and fund managers in other countries also generally confirm the relative insignificance of theoretically-based analysis methods in domestic share appraisal (e.g., Arnold *et al.* (1984) and Block (1999) in the US; Vergoossen (1993) in the Netherlands; and Olbert (1994) in Sweden).

4.3.4 Economic Value Added

Economic Value Added (EVA®) is a relatively new technique registered as a trademark by the Stern-Stewart consulting group. It essentially involves adjusting accounting earnings to a standard measure (involving up to 120 adjustments) and reducing these earnings to allow for a charge for the cost of capital. EVA is therefore formulated upon the notion of economic profit, or residual income, i.e., the amount of profit which can be consumed without eroding the firm's capital. Hence, despite its apparent novelty, the origins of EVA can be traced at least as far back as the 1930s (e.g., Preinreich, 1938; Hicks, 1939).

The prevalence of EVA among the investment community has yet to be investigated. When introduced, EVA was initially lauded as a superior performance measure to traditional accounting-based measures. However, it has since attracted criticism for the *ad hoc* nature of the accounting adjustments and for discouraging investment due to the effects of low revenues and capital charges in early years (e.g. O'Hanlon and Peasnell, 1998). In an empirical study of the links between EVA and stock market data for 773 companies, Biddle *et al.* (1997) find no evidence to support claims that EVA is more closely associated with equity returns or firm values than traditional accounting earnings. In fact, they note (1997, pp. 331–332):

> There is little evidence to support the Stern Stewart claim that EVA is superior to earnings in its association with stock returns or firm values. In no case does EVA significantly outperform [earnings before extraordinary items] in tests of relative information content. On the contrary, in most cases the evidence suggests that earnings outperforms EVA.

O'Hanlon and Peasnell (1998) also point out that EVA should not be used in isolation, as the extent to which it accurately captures a company's value is affected by the degree of balance sheet conservatism. They demonstrate that companies whose balance sheet is conservative (and thus under-represents true value) will result in high positive future expected EVA values and vice versa. Given that the degree of balance sheet conservatism varies considerably between industries (e.g., pharmaceutical companies typically have higher than average intangible assets not captured by the balance sheet), and between countries (see Chapter 3), caution must be exercised when comparing EVA data across sectors and across countries.

4.3.5 Top-down analysis

In the context of overseas investment, the top-down analysis approach is where funds are allocated to countries on the basis of economic variables. Individual company investment decisions are then made within the fund allocated to each country. This has the advantage of avoiding international comparisons of accounting information on individual companies. An important assumption of top-down analysis is that the correlation between different countries' equity returns is low, i.e., it assumes segmented capital markets. Country-effects are therefore assumed to be more important than industry effects in a top-down approach. However recent evidence challenges this assumption. For example, UBS Brinson (2000) show that industry factors are becoming more dominant while Bilson *et al.* (2001) demonstrate that national boundaries are of diminishing importance.

In a study by the US Association for Investment Management and Research, Hopkins and Miller (2001) examine the relative contribution of country, sector and company factors in global portfolio management. Using the Morgan Stanley Capital International (MSCI) industry classification, they conclude (p. 63) that:

> A relatively significant shift appears to have recently occurred in the importance of global sectors and industries at the expense of geography in global investment strategies. Although this emphasis can and does shift through time, the rewards from global sector allocation, as well as organizing stock selection on sectoral lines, seems to justify allocating resources to sector research on an ongoing basis.

Given these findings, the popularity of top-down analysis is likely to wane over time, as international markets look likely to continue to integrate.

A final point worth noting is that while the empirical studies discussed in this chapter have been considered as pertaining solely to domestic equity analysis, not all the above studies *explicitly* specify that overseas company analysis is excluded. For example, whereas Arnold and Moizer (1984) and Moizer and Arnold (1984) remove from their sample respondents involved in overseas securities, some studies make no such distinction. However, given that the statistics in Chapter 2 show that the vast majority of funds are held in domestic securities (especially in the US), the techniques analysed will overwhelmingly refer to domestic decisions. It is also possible to infer from certain studies that the intention of the research is to investigate domestic decision making specifically as the results of the techniques used are related by the authors to the specific characteristics of the domestic equity market (e.g., Pike *et al.*, 1993; Vergoossen, 1993; Olbert, 1994; Wong and Cheung, 1999). Finally, in the case of studies that have used experimental methodologies (such as Biggs, 1984; Bouwman *et al.*, 1987; Hunton and McEwen, 1997), the financial information provided to participants relates to domestic companies and, as such, the findings are specific to that decision-making domain.

4.4 THE EFFICIENT MARKETS HYPOTHESIS AND EQUITY ANALYSIS TECHNIQUES

When considering the extent to which particular appraisal techniques are adopted in practice, it is important to consider stock market informational efficiency. In general, the Efficient Markets Hypothesis (EMH) asserts that, given certain assumptions, security prices instantaneously and fully reflect all relevant publicly available information. Thus, persistent deviations of security prices from their fair or fundamental values will not exceed transaction costs.

EMH can be assessed at three levels of efficiency: weak form, semi-strong form and strong form (Fama, 1970). Weak form efficiency implies that share prices reflect all available, relevant past information. Therefore, if stock markets are weak form efficient, technical analysis should theoretically yield no profits, as this information will have already been impounded into the share price. Semi-strong efficiency implies that current share prices instantaneously and fully reflect all relevant publicly available information, while the strong form version of the EMH states that prices instantaneously and fully reflect all relevant information, including 'insider' information (Blake, 2000).

There has been a great deal of empirical research on the EMH, but overall, the evidence remains inconclusive. While early studies provide evidence that most developed stock markets are at least semi-strong form efficient, (e.g., Fama, 1970; Jensen, 1978), more recent research documents the profitability of trading strategies based on analysis of previous share price movements. Rouwenhorst (1997) and Chan *et al.* (2000), for example, showed how momentum strategies (i.e., picking past 'winners' and selling past 'losers') implemented on international stock markets yielded abnormal profits.

Against this background, contemporary finance research is increasingly beginning to acknowledge the limitations of the EMH. Shleifer (2000), in particular, provides a comprehensive refutation of the EMH, arguing that 'behavioural finance' models offer a far better explanation of previous empirical findings. Shleifer cites numerous anomalies which would not exist under efficient markets, such as De Bondt and Thaler's (1985) finding that risk adjusted profits can be made by investing in companies which have performed well over the previous three years, and selling short companies which have performed well over the same horizon.

One explanation propounded by Shleifer for arbitrage failing to enforce the EMH in such situations is 'noise trader' risk. This risk is where mispricing of shares becomes more, rather than less, acute in the short run. Hence, arbitrageurs risk being unable to finance their activities over the duration of the share's deviation from its fundamental value. Such risks may well be realistic if the mispricing persists for months, or even years, as is often the case (e.g., see Froot and Dabora, 1999).

It is important to note, however, that the techniques used by analysts and investors are more a function of *beliefs* about market efficiency, rather than *actual* market efficiency. If analysts do not believe the market to be weak form efficient, then (irrespective of whether the market actually is or is not) they are likely to perceive technical analysis as useful because they do not believe that all past information is reflected in current security prices. Similarly, if analysts do not believe the market to be semi-strong efficient, then they are likely to perceive fundamental analysis as useful as they do not believe that all current publicly available information is reflected in current security prices.

In general, research indicates that analysts believe the markets do not reflect all publicly available information. For example, Mayer-Sommer (1979) found that analysts have far more faith in the market being weak form efficient than semi-strong efficient. Whereas 44% accepted research findings relating to EMH in weak form, only 2% did so for semi-strong form efficiency. Moreover, whereas only 57% of analysts perceived technical analysis as being useful in achieving excess returns over the long term, 99% believed fundamental analysis to be useful for this purpose.

More recently, Carter and Van Auken (1990) found that fund managers reject the EMH in all forms except for weak form efficiency, while Block (1999) found that less than 3% of analysts strongly agree with the EMH in its semi-strong form.[3] The relative importance attached to fundamental analysis and technical analysis is therefore at least a partial reflection of analysts' and fund managers' views of market informational efficiency.

[3] Gniewosz (1990) points out that some analysts believe that research into the EMH ignores market psychology (i.e., where the reaction to news is at least partly contingent upon the general market conditions), which may explain why there is not a great deal of acceptance of semi-strong efficiency.

4.5 EXISTING EMPIRICAL EVIDENCE ON TRANSNATIONAL EQUITY ANALYSIS

Despite the significant growth in cross-border investment outlined in Chapter 2, various commentators have acknowledged our lack of knowledge of cross-border equity decisions (e.g., Hopwood, 1994). The earliest study to investigate this issue was conducted by Choi and Levich (1991). They interviewed 52 institutional investors, corporate issuers, investment underwriters and market regulators drawn from New York, London, Zurich, Frankfurt and Tokyo. They recognised that although financial decisions are increasingly international in scope, financial statements are typically prepared according to local accounting standards. Choi and Levich found that some investors avoided earnings-based information and some abandoned discounted future earnings models (i.e. fundamental analysis) in favour of the discounted cash flow model. Others relied either on macroeconomic variables (i.e., a top-down approach) or on data on consumer preferences, because of differences in international accounting.

In a survey of 44 US and 14 UK fund managers involved in transnational investment, Bhushan and Lessard (1992) found that almost 80% of UK investors considered themselves 'top-down' managers at the country level, thus minimising the need for company specific information. At the individual company level, 62% saw themselves as 'bottom-up' managers, requiring extensive company information.

Bhushan and Lessard (1992) note that in general, fund managers do not avoid international investing due to accounting diversity and rely on comparisons with a firm's own history and with other local firms in the same industry. Therefore, accounting diversity appears to be significant enough to affect the choice of techniques used in foreign equity analysis, but not substantial enough to warrant avoiding investment in certain foreign companies altogether. What is unclear is whether capital market integration has affected the reliance on top-down analysis, since Bhushan and Lessard's study was based on data collected in the late 1980s.

In an interview survey of 17 analysts and fund managers based in London, Miles and Nobes (1998) found that although some fund managers and analysts used non-accounting analysis techniques (such as trend analysis and reliance on macroeconomic data) ratio analysis was widely used, especially the P/E ratio. Not all interviewees were able to choose which countries they analysed as the countries were allocated to them. However, three fund managers said that they did avoid certain countries, especially those with weak accounting regulation. As pointed out by Miles and Nobes (1998), this could well lead to an increased cost of capital for companies in such countries if investors perceive their accounting information to be of poor quality.

The most recent study of this issue was conducted by Marton (1998), who focuses on Swedish companies as providers of accounting information, but studies non-Swedish analysts and investors (based in London, New York and Frankfurt) as recipients and users of this information. Marton found that fundamental analysis was the most popular technique of analysis – all analysts interviewed used this approach. Marton also found that analysts are affected by their national context, as there were some differences between German methods of analysis on the one hand, and US and UK methods on the other. In particular, he found that German analysts tend to have a longer term focus, while UK analysts and fund managers were more focused on corporate governance issues than US and German analysts.

4.6 SUMMARY

This chapter has reviewed the research into the analysis of domestic and foreign equities by investors and analysts. Relative to the wealth of research into domestic analysis, cross-border equity analysis has received very little attention by the academic community.

Prior research reveals that fundamental analysis is clearly the most influential technique in domestic equity valuation. This result holds over time, across countries, between professional groups and across research methodologies. The secondary status of technical analysis and the theoretically-based techniques such as beta analysis and DCF analysis is also a consistent finding of prior research. Although market efficiency would predict a limited role for technical analysis, the theoretical appeal of DCF techniques would imply more widespread use.

As noted earlier in this chapter, the definition of fundamental analysis is often ambiguous. Consequently, fundamental analysis may involve reliance on many sources of information. The following chapter therefore examines the research into the information sources used by analysts and fund managers when analysing ordinary shares.

4.7 REFERENCES

Arnold, J. and Moizer, P. (1984). 'A survey of the methods used by UK investment analysts to appraise investments in ordinary shares.' *Accounting and Business Research*, **Summer**, 195–207.

Arnold, J., Moizer, P and Noreen, E. (1984). 'Investment appraisal methods of financial analysts: a comparative study of US and UK practices.' *International Journal of Accounting*, **Spring**, 1–18.

Barker, R. (1999a). 'The role of dividends in valuation models used by analysts and fund managers.' *The European Accounting Review*, **8** (2), 195–218.
Barker, R. (1999b). 'Survey and market-based evidence of industry-dependence in analysts' preferences between the dividend yield and price-earnings ratio valuation models.' *Journal of Business Finance and Accounting*, **26** (3), 393–418.
Bauman, M.P. (1996). 'A review of fundamental analysis research in accounting.' *Journal of Accounting Literature*, **15**, 1–33.
Bhushan, R. and Lessard, D.R. (1992). 'Coping with international accounting diversity: fund managers' views on disclosure, reconciliation, and harmonization.' *Journal of International Financial Management and Accounting*, **4** (2), 149–164.
Biddle, G.C, Bowen, R.M. and Wallace, J.S. (1997). 'Does EVA beat earnings? Evidence on associations with stock returns and firm values.' *Journal of Accounting and Economics*, **24** (3), 301–336.
Biggs, S.F. (1984). 'Financial analysts' information search in the assessment of corporate earning power.' *Accounting, Organizations and Society*, **9** (3/4), 313–323.
Bilson, C.M., Brailsford, T.J. and Hooper, V.J. (2001). 'Selecting macroeconomic variables as explanatory factors of emerging stock market returns.' *Pacific Basin Finance Journal*, **9**, 401–426.
Blake, D. (2000). *Financial Market Analysis*, 2nd edn, John Wiley and Sons, Chichester.
Block, S.B. (1999). 'A study of financial analysts: practice and theory.' *Financial Analysts Journal*, **July/August**, 86–95.
Bouwman, M., Frishkoff, P.A. and Frishkoff, P. (1987). 'How do financial analysts make decisions? A process model of the investment screening decision.' *Accounting, Organizations and Society*, **12** (1), 1–29.
Carter, R.B. and Van Auken, H.E. (1990). 'Security analysis and portfolio management: a survey and analysis.' *Journal of Portfolio Management*, **Spring**, 81–85.
Chan, K., Hameed, A. and Tong, W. (2000). 'Profitability of momentum strategies in the international equity markets.' *Journal of Financial and Quantitative Analysis*, **35** (2), 153–172.
Choi, F.D.S. and Levich, R.M. (1991). 'Behavioral effects of international accounting diversity.' *Accounting Horizons*, **June**, 1–13.
De Bondt, W.F.M. and Thaler, R. (1985). 'Does the stock market overreact?' *Journal of Finance*, **40**, 793–805.
Edwards, R.D., Magee, J. and Bassetti, W.H.C. (2001) *Technical Analysis of Stock Trends*, 8th Edn, St. Lucie Press, Washington D.C.
Fama, E.F. (1970). 'Efficient capital markets: a review of theory and empirical work.' *Journal of Finance*, **25** (2), 383–417.
Firth, M. (1977). *The Valuation of Shares and the Efficient Markets Theory*. Macmillan Press, London.
Foley, B.J. (1991). *Capital Markets*. Macmillan, London.
Froot, K.A. and Dabora, E. (1999). 'How are stock process affected by the location of trade?' *Journal of Financial Economics*, **53** (2), 189–216.
Gniewosz, G. (1990). 'The share investment decision process and information use: an exploratory case study.' *Accounting and Business Research*, **20** (79), 223–230.
Hicks, J.R. (1939). *Value and Capital*. Oxford University Press, London.
Hopkins, P.J.B. and Miller, C.H. (2001). *Country, Sector and Company Factors in Global Equity Portfolios*, Association for Investment Management and Research, Charlottesville, Virginia.

Hopwood, A.G. (1994). 'Some reflections on "The Harmonization of Accounting Within the EU".' *The European Accounting Review*, **3** (2), 241–253.

Hunton, J.E. and McEwen, R.A. (1997). 'An assessment of the relation between analysts' earnings forecast accuracy, motivational incentives and information search strategy.' *The Accounting Review*, **72** (4), 497–515.

Jensen, M.C. (1978). 'Some anomalous evidence regarding market efficiency.' *Journal of Financial Economics*, **6**, 95–102.

Lundholm, R.J. (1995). 'A tutorial on the Ohlson and Feltham/Ohlson models: answers to some frequently asked questions.' *Contemporary Accounting Research*, **4**, 27–46.

Marton, J. (1998). *Accounting and Stock Markets: A Study of Swedish Accounting for International Investors and Analysts*, BAS, Gothenburg University, Sweden.

Mayer-Sommer, A. (1979). 'Understanding and acceptance of the efficient markets hypothesis and its accounting implications.' *The Accounting Review*, **54** (1), 88–106.

Miles, S. and Nobes, C. (1998). 'The use of foreign accounting data in UK financial institutions.' *Journal of Business Finance and Accounting*, **25** (3 and 4), 309–328.

Miller, M.H. and Modigliani, F. (1961). 'Dividend policy, growth and the valuation of shares.' *Journal of Business*, **XXXIV**(4), 411–433.

Moizer, P. and Arnold, J. (1984). 'Share appraisal by investment analysts – portfolio vs. non-portfolio managers.' *Accounting and Business Research*, **Autumn**, 341–348.

O'Hanlon, J. and Peasnell, K. (1998). 'Wall Street's contribution to management accounting: the Stern Stewart EVA financial management system.' *Management Accounting Research*, **9** (4), 421–444.

Ohlson, J.A. (1995). 'Earnings, book value and dividends in equity valuation.' *Contemporary Accounting Research*, **11**, 749–761.

Olbert, L. (1994). 'Stock valuation methods of financial analysts in a thin stock market in Sweden, with comparisons to the United Kingdom and the United States.' *International Journal of Accounting*, **29**, 123–135.

Penman, S.H. (1992) 'Return to fundamentals.' *Journal of Accounting, Auditing and Finance*, **7**, 465–483.

Peasnell, K.V. (1982). 'Some formal connections between economic yields and values and accounting numbers.' *Journal of Business Finance and Accounting*, **9** (3), 361–381.

Pike, R., Meerjanssen, J. and Chadwick, L. (1993). 'The appraisal of ordinary shares by investment analysts in the UK and Germany.' *Accounting and Business Research*, **23** (92), 489–499.

Preinreich, G. (1938). 'Annual survey of economic theory: the theory of depreciation.' *Econometrica*, **6** (3), 219–241.

Roll, R. (1977) 'A critique of the asset pricing theory's test: part I.' *Journal of Financial Economics*, **4**, 129–176.

Rouwenhorst, K.G. (1997). 'International momentum strategies.' *Journal of Finance*, **53**, 267–284.

Rutterford, J. (2004). 'From dividend yield to discounted cash flow: a history of UK and US equity valuation techniques.' *Accounting, Business and Financial History* **14** (2), 115–149.

Shleifer, A. (2000) *Inefficient Markets: An Introduction to Behavioral Finance*. Oxford University Press, Oxford.

UBS Brinson (2000). *Equity Portfolio Management: The Dominance of Industry Factors*, UBS Asset Management.

Vergoossen, R. (1993). 'The use and perceived importance of annual reports by investment analysts in the Netherlands.' *The European Accounting Review*, **2**, 219–244.

Wong, M.C. and Cheung, Y.L. (1999). 'The practice of investment management in Hong Kong: market forecasting and stock selection.' *OMEGA*, **27**, 451–465.

5 Information Sources Used in Equity Analysis

5.1 INTRODUCTION

The previous chapter indicated that fundamental analysis is the dominant approach to valuing equities by analysts and fund managers in a domestic context. However, it was also pointed out that the formal definition of fundamental analysis is often unclear; informally it entails the analysis of firm-specific factors and wider industry and macro-economic factors to arrive at an intrinsic value for the firm. This chapter aims to clarify which factors are the important ones in determining firm value in a domestic context by reviewing the relevant academic literature on the sources of information used in equity decision making. It also reviews the limited research into transnational equity analysis.

The chapter shows that both theory and empirical evidence are in agreement that accounting information is an important determinant of equity prices. In recent years, however, direct communications between financial institutions and company management, such as management meetings and company visits, have displaced the annual report as the most influential information source.

The remainder of this chapter first examines the role of accounting information in domestic equity analysis and then reviews the empirical evidence on the increasing reliance of fund managers and analysts on direct communications with company management. There has been relatively little research into the information relied upon by analysts and fund managers in transnational equity analysis; this research forms the basis of the penultimate section. The final section summarises the chapter.

5.2 THE USEFULNESS OF ANNUAL REPORTS AND ACCOUNTING INFORMATION

5.2.1 The theoretical case for the relevance of accounting information

Empirical research in the UK spanning over 20 years has shown that accounting information is one of the principal sources of information used by investors and analysts in domestic equity analysis. Despite having an established history[1], attempts to establish a *theoretical* relationship between accounting numbers and economic values of companies have been controversial. Many commentators continue to insist that anything other than risk adjusted cash flows is irrelevant to equity valuation. Accounting is viewed as a record-keeping exercise and the outputs of the double-entry accounting system are deemed to be entirely irrelevant to the value of the firm. Others have made the more moderate criticism that accounting profits or book values are relevant only to the extent that they are useful for providing information about future cash flows (see Penman (1992) for examples of, and responses to, such criticisms).

The theory of accounting and equity valuation developed by Peasnell (1982) and Ohlson (1989; 1990; 1991), however, posits a central role for financial statement data, rather than as a mere proxy for cash flow. These authors show that provided the 'clean surplus' relation applies, market value can be *defined* in terms of book value, earnings and capital charges. They also show that a model based on such variables can be reconciled to the dividend discount model described in Chapter 4. The clean surplus relation requires the change in book value to be equivalent to prior period book value, plus earnings, less dividends, thus:

$$BV_t = BV_{t-1} + X_t - d_t \tag{5.1}$$

where BV_t represents book value at time t, X_t represents accounting earnings in year t, and d_t represents dividends paid in year t (all on a per share basis and where capital contributions are treated as negative dividends). If this relation holds, Peasnell (1982) and Ohlson (1990) show that, irrespective of the accounting policies adopted by companies for items such as depreciation and research and development, share price at time $t(P_t)$ can be defined by the following equation:

$$P_t = BV_t + \sum_{\tau=1}^{\infty} \frac{E(X_{t+\tau} - BV_t k)}{(1+k)^{\tau}} \tag{5.2}$$

where k represents the cost of capital. Thus, the value of a share is equal to the book value per share, plus the discounted value of expected earnings (based on information available at time t) after a charge on beginning of period book value has been made at the cost of capital.[2] Therefore, the balance sheet (which captures book value) and the profit and loss account

[1] For example, as noted by Lundholm (1995) and Barker (1999), the model presented in this section was originally presented in Preinreich (1938).

[2] Note that this model is what underpins Stern Stewart's EVA® approach to equity analysis discussed in Chapter 4.

(which captures earnings) should be useful in identifying securities that are over or under-valued.

5.2.2 Empirical evidence on the use of accounting information in domestic equity analysis

5.2.2.1 UK research

In line with the theory outlined above, empirical research into the information used by UK analysts and fund managers consistently shows that accounting information is heavily used in domestic equity analysis. In their UK study, Lee and Tweedie (1981) found that, along with the interim statements, the annual report was the most important source of information to fund managers. In particular, the profit and loss account and balance sheet were read thoroughly by 90% of respondents. Similarly, Arnold and Moizer (1984) identified the profit and loss account as the most influential information source used by UK analysts and fund managers. The balance sheet was the next most important information source, followed by interim results.

The annual report has also been found to play a reference role. In a study of fifteen UK investment analysts, Day (1986) found that although the annual report was not considered a timely source, it was nevertheless vital in the decision-making process, as analysts review it upon receipt, read it thoroughly at their leisure and refer to it throughout the year. The items referred to most frequently by analysts were long term debt, the balance sheet and profits. However, because Day's approach involved no other sources of information, it was not possible to ascertain the *relative* importance of the annual report.

Further evidence for the 'reference' role for the annual report is provided by Holland (1998). He found that, along with other components of the reporting cycle, the annual report forms the structure around which disclosure in meetings with investors is organised. Holland found that both the financial statements and narrative information were used as a benchmark against which future performance was to be judged: 'The case companies argued that if the financial report did not exist the users such as [financial institutions] would lack a baseline to see how the future evolved' (Holland 1998, p. 265). Thus, despite primarily containing historical information, the annual report is therefore still useful to investors for the future predictions upon which their decisions are based.

5.2.2.2 Differences between analysts and fund managers

Because of the differences between analysts' and fund managers' roles outlined in Chapter 2, research is increasingly treating these two groups as heterogeneous in their use of various information sources, including accounting information. In the first study to fully acknowledge the differences, Moizer and Arnold (1984) found that analysts generally used most sources more often than fund managers. They attributed this to the fact that analysts are not required to manage a portfolio and therefore devote more time and effort to equity analysis *per se*. Annual reports and interim reports were used significantly more by analysts, and fund managers were found to rely more on other analysts as they performed less frequent and less detailed analysis themselves. Analysts also made more use of discussions with company personnel.

Using cluster analysis, Bence *et al.* (1995) also detected significant differences between fund managers and investment analysts, although accounting information was deemed important to both groups. The predominant cluster of information sources for investment analysts included preliminary statements, interim statements, annual reports, company presentations and personal interviews. Fund managers, by contrast, were found to rely more heavily on company visits, preliminary and interim statements and personal interviews. The clusters (which are proxies for the groups of information sources) indicated that analysts tend to use routinely acquired information, whereas investors prefer to use actively acquired information.

In the most recent and most detailed examination of this issue, Barker (1998) found that the interim results and the annual report differed in importance for sell-side analysts, finance directors and fund managers. Although finance directors did not think the annual report constituted 'news', it was seen as useful in its role as a public relations document and, consistent with Holland (1998), formed the basis of a track record. Analysts ranked the annual report behind personal managerial contact and results announcements. Barker attributes analysts' preference for managerial contact over the annual report to their short-term 'news' orientation. Fund managers attached more importance to the annual report than analysts did, ranking it behind only formal meetings with company management.

5.2.3 Annual reports and the Efficient Markets Hypothesis

Although prior research demonstrates that the annual report and financial statements are considered useful in analysts' and investors' decision making, they rarely address the intriguing question of why this is the case when considered in light of the Efficient Markets Hypothesis (EMH). As Hines (1982) points out, the evidence supportive of the EMH implies that annual reports cannot be used by shareholders to make abnormal profits for two reasons. First, because the annual report is publicly available and therefore the information contained in it is immediately impounded into the share price on release; and second, because the preliminary statements precede the annual report and convey much of the information to the market weeks before the annual report is published. Therefore, the annual report should contain no new information.

One reason for this apparent conflict is that the annual report is not necessarily used as a short-term information source, i.e., it does not contain price sensitive information. The results of Holland (1998) and Barker (1998) are consistent with this contention. Furthermore, as discussed in Chapter 4, much recent research provides evidence that challenges the notion of market efficiency (e.g., Shleifer, 2000).

An alternative theoretical view of stock markets' interpretation and use of accounting information is provided by Hand (1990). Hand moderates the EMH and extends the 'functional fixation hypothesis' (which posits that users of accounting information cannot unravel the true economic implications of accounting information),[3] contending that share prices may be set by either sophisticated or unsophisticated investors. The former will be aware of the cash flow implications of accounting data, whereas the latter will not. This hypothesis implies that the share price response to the release of accounting information will be contingent upon the likelihood that share prices will be set by an unsophisticated investor. In an empirical study of market reactions to announcements of swap transactions that had no real economic implications, Hand found evidence inconsistent with the EMH, but in line with the extended functional fixation hypothesis. Specifically, he found that the reaction to the announcements was contingent upon the level of institutional ownership (a proxy for the relative proportions of sophisticated and unsophisticated investors). However, Tinic (1990) challenges Hand's view by pointing out that any valuation errors made by unsophisticated investors should be exploited by their sophisticated counterparts via arbitrage trading.[4]

Irrespective of the predictions of the EMH, prior research shows clearly that the annual report and the financial statements represent a primary information source. However, the validity and relevance of accounting information has been questioned in recent years. For example, Beattie (2000) points to the lack of timeliness and the historic focus of accounting information as areas of financial reporting which sit uncomfortably with the contemporary business environment. Against this background, therefore, it

[3] Such a view is consistent with Breton and Taffler (1995), who found that analysts did not adjust accounts for creative accounting policies.

[4] Ball and Kothari (1991) also express reservations about Hand's empirical findings, attributing them to size factors. However, Hand (1991) addresses some of their concerns in a response.

is unsurprising that accounting information is increasingly augmented by analysts and fund managers by other information sources, especially contact with company management.

5.3 DIRECT COMPANY CONTACT AS AN INFORMATION SOURCE

Analysis of research into the information used by UK analysts and fund managers in domestic analysis reveals a shift over time in the importance attached to direct company contact *vis-à-vis* the annual report. In particular, contact with company personnel, especially meetings with management, has increased in importance in the last two decades or so. Lee and Tweedie (1981) found that company visits were the next most influential source *after* the annual report. Three years later, Arnold and Moizer (1984) found that the profit and loss account, balance sheet and interim results were all considered more influential than discussions with company personnel. However, Arnold and Moizer speculated that the importance of company discussions may have been understated in their own study. This is because they felt that respondents may have feared that 'disclosure of the true importance could result in suspicions of "insider trading" being used with a consequent increase in the probability of such use being effectively controlled' (Arnold and Moizer, 1984 p. 203). Despite the perceived influence of management in their appraisal of ordinary shares, respondents displayed a degree of scepticism regarding the reliability of managerial communication, either due to a perceived lack of understanding, or managers deliberately attempting to 'steer' analysts towards conservative forecasts.[5]

In the next study of this issue, Pike *et al.* (1993) found that the annual report and interim reports were ranked as the third most important information source *behind* discussions with company personnel and company meetings. Marston (1993) also found that large companies devote considerable resources to investor relations, and that meetings with analysts and fund managers were the most important means of communication. Barker (1998) reported that analysts and fund managers regarded direct company contact in the form of company visits, meetings with management or analysts meetings as significantly more important than the annual report, even though in a later paper based on the same data it was acknowledged that the analytical process was anchored in accounting information (Barker, 1999).

[5] Such behaviour is designed to enable management to exceed analysts' forecasts and thus demonstrate to shareholders that they have outperformed the market's expectations.

Marston (1999) also found that sell-side analysts, fund managers, finance directors and investor relations managers all consider company meetings to be important. Although meetings with management are often perceived as costly because of the time required, Marston found that all parties perceived such meetings as highly beneficial: companies themselves were able to gauge market sentiment, while analysts and investors gained from improved liquidity in the shares and fair share price setting by the market.

It is possible that research showing the annual report to be falling in importance relative to company contact is attributable to analysts and investors becoming less reticent about admitting the significance of disclosure from company personnel over time, rather than an actual increase in the importance of these meetings. However, evidence indicates that the increasing importance is more likely to reflect increasing reliance on company personnel as a key information source. For example, Marston (1999) found that between 1991 and 1996, there was an average increase of 63% in the number of one-to-one meetings held by companies. Furthermore, the number of sell-side analysts and fund managers held on company circulation lists for invitations to meetings increased by 66% and 58%, respectively. Companies are therefore encouraging such contact by devoting increasingly substantial resources to investor relations.

5.4 INTERNATIONAL EVIDENCE ON INFORMATION SOURCES USED IN DOMESTIC EQUITY ANALYSIS

Research into the sources of information used by analysts and fund managers in domestic equity analysis has by no means been confined to the UK. Although some differences between analysts of different nationality have been identified, overall, most international research is consistent with the UK evidence that accounting information and contact with management are the most useful sources. For example, the comparative international research of Arnold *et al.* (1984) found significant differences in the importance of eight out of fifteen information sources used by analysts from the UK and US. Both groups regarded the profit and loss account and balance sheet as the most influential sources, although US analysts considered these financial statements more influential than their UK counterparts. Managerial contact was also considered relatively more important by UK analysts. Furthermore, while Pike *et al.* (1993) found that British analysts ranked discussion with company personnel as their most important information source, followed by analysts' in-company meetings, then annual reports, German analysts rated in-company meetings as their most important source, with annual reports ranked second.

In line with the model presented in equation (5.2), Govindarajan (1980) found that US analysts rely more heavily on accounting earnings than on cash flow, despite the Financial Accounting Standards Board (FASB) in the US prescribing the reporting of cash flow information for investment decisions. Using content analysis, Govindarajan tested the hypothesis that analysts are more interested in earnings information than in cash flow information. He found that of 976 analysts' reports examined, 845 (87%) had an earnings emphasis and attached more importance to earnings rather than cash flows, which was only more important in 28 (fewer than 3%) of cases.

In fact, reliance of US fund managers and analysts on accounting information is a persistent finding. In a more recent content analysis of US analysts' reports, Previts *et al.* (1994) found that analysts focus primarily on income rather than on balance sheet or cash flow in their recommendations, although analysts give more attention to balance sheet items for thinly-traded and poorly-understood companies. Balance sheet information also featured in analysts' reports, mainly relating to assets, capital, debt and equity. Analysts also extensively consider non-financial information, such as market share, industry factors and the recent financial history of the company, consistent with use of fundamental analysis. Finally, and in line with UK findings, Previts *et al.*, confirm that analysts rely heavily on management for information about their companies, and consider the quality of management in their analyses.

Similar results have been found for European analysts. Vergoossen (1993) found that in the Netherlands, the most recent annual report was considered the most important information source, while communications with managers and interim reports were ranked second and third respectively. The most important individual components of the annual report were the financial statements, with the income statement and the balance sheet ranking ahead of the footnotes. In a study of 273 Swedish analysts, Olbert (1994) showed that the financial statements are the most influential components of the annual report, followed by interim results, notes to the accounts and company personnel. Of the financial statements, the balance sheet and profit and loss account ranked as the first and second most influential sources respectively.

Finally, both Anderson (1981) and Gniewosz (1990) found that the annual report was the most important information source to institutional investors in Australia. Indeed, Gniewosz (1990) concluded that the receipt of the annual report was the major routine information event of the financial year.

5.5 EXISTING EMPIRICAL EVIDENCE ON TRANSNATIONAL INFORMATION SOURCES

As noted in the introduction, there has been a lack of research into the information used in cross-border equity analysis. This lack of research is increasingly conspicuous in light of the significant growth in institutional investors and cross-border investment outlined in Chapter 2. The limited number of studies into the information sources used by analysts and fund managers in transnational equity analysis have focused only on the use of accounting information. Thus, no previous studies have considered the wider information set available to analysts and fund managers, such as company visits and management meetings. Two main approaches have been adopted to investigate this issue: survey-based and market-based.

5.5.1 Survey-based research

The earliest survey on the use of overseas accounting information was conducted by Choi and Levich (1991). They conducted interviews with 52 institutional investors, corporate issuers, investment underwriters and market regulators drawn from Frankfurt, London, New York, Tokyo and Zurich. Their main finding was that about half of respondents felt that accounting diversity affected their capital market decisions. Over half of the institutional investors involved in the study (9 out of 17) stated that accounting differences made it more difficult for them to measure their decision variables and therefore ultimately affected their investment decisions. The remainder adopted investment techniques which did not require the use of annual reports, indicating that accounting information on foreign firms is, on average, less useful than for domestic firms.

The extent to which respondents' decisions were affected differed substantially: of the institutions stating that accounting diversity represents a problem, seven coped by restating accounts to a familiar base, two adopted different investment strategies and one restricted investment to government bonds. Those who claimed that accounting diversity did not pose a problem adopted a variety of investment approaches, including the adoption of a 'multiple principles capability' (which involves becoming familiar with local accounting principles) and using macro economic variables for country comparisons, then investing in a portfolio in the selected countries (i.e., a 'top down' approach). Interestingly, Choi and Levich's research indicated that the country of domicile was a potential factor determining the usefulness of accounting information. Japan, Germany and Switzerland were cited most frequently as countries whose accounting principles were a source of concern for analysts investing overseas.

Bhushan and Lessard (1992) found that while international UK and US investors viewed SEC-required reconciliations and more uniform disclosures and harmonisation positively, they did not regard them as critical in the investment process. Difficulty in comparing accounting earnings across countries was considered the greatest obstacle to cross border valuations. Accordingly, more uniform disclosures, reconciliations to US GAAP and international harmonisation were all viewed positively by fund managers.

Two more recent studies of accounting information involving UK fund managers and analysts are Miles and Nobes (1998) and Marton (1998). In their survey of 17 analysts and fund managers based in London, Miles and Nobes (1998) examined how accounting data are used and the impact of accounting diversity on foreign equity analysis. In line with Choi and Levich (1991), approximately half of the interviewees in Miles and Nobes perceived themselves to be affected by international accounting differences. However, sector experts were more affected than country experts. Most of the analysts specialising by country stated that they were unaffected by accounting diversity, indicating that international comparability (or lack of comparability) of accounting information is important to analysts.

Miles and Nobes found that of the 17 interviewees, only six adjusted the accounts; one of whom substantially restated the accounts. Moreover, the fund managers assumed that analysts adjusted the accounts, although only 56% of analysts interviewed did actually adjust.

Marton (1998) found that despite its historical focus, accounting information was still relevant to investors in a transnational context, as analysts and investors face uncertainty over the *present* position of the firm. Therefore, even though accounting information relates to past economic activity, it is still seen as relevant to this uncertainty. Out of fifteen analysts interviewed, four regarded the annual report as essential and nine used it with other information sources. These respondents also indicated that the profit and loss account and balance sheet are important in foreign equity analysis. However, although analysts were interested in cash flows, the reported statement of cash flows was not seen as necessarily relevant, due to variations in the definition of reported cash flow.

Interestingly, when asked about the desirability of the international harmonisation of accounting standards, analysts overwhelmingly responded positively. Of the fifteen analysts interviewed, thirteen stated that they saw harmonisation as desirable, one said that it was undesirable and one did not respond. Finally, Marton found that the information used by analysts depends on where the analyst is based. He found that US analysts made more use of US GAAP, whereas European analysts made more use of local standards.

Prior survey-based research into transnational analysis therefore indicates that accounting differences do have an impact upon the analysis of foreign equities. The extent of this impact, however, is unclear. Also unclear is the *relative* importance attached to accounting information given the research which shows that alternative information sources are useful in a domestic context (e.g. company contact). The following section reviews the findings of market-based attempts to shed further light on these issues.

5.5.2 Market-based evidence on transnational equity analysis

Research into the usefulness of foreign accounting data to investors shares many characteristics with the international market based research discussed in Chapter 3. However, the key difference is that the following studies assess the relevance of the accounting figures of companies domiciled in a different country to the stock market where share prices are examined. That is, to the extent that stock exchange trading is conducted by local investors, the users of the accounting information are located in a different country to the reporting company. This research therefore assesses the reactions of investors to foreign (i.e., transnational) accounting information.

Due to the availability of SEC reconciliation data in Form 20-F, prior research is exclusively based on US stock markets. These data are particularly useful to researchers as two sets of accounting data for each company can be analysed, hence they provide a unique opportunity to use each company as its own 'control'. This eliminates any extraneous factors which can confound the analysis when comparing accounting data for different companies.

Two main methodologies have been used to examine the usefulness of foreign accounting data. The first is where the market reaction to foreign (i.e., non-US) data and reconciliation (i.e., US GAAP-based) data is tested in order to ascertain whether this information impacts upon investors and share prices. Abnormal share returns are examined on two days – the first is where the earnings announcement based on local accounting principles was made; the second when the US GAAP reconciliations were made available. The second (and most common) methodology is where the value relevance of the accounting reconciliations is tested in order to assess whether this information is used by investors in setting share prices.[6]

Meek (1983) represents the earliest attempt to examine whether investors use foreign accounting data. Meek assessed the impact of international

[6] See Chapter 3 for more details on the definition of value relevance.

accounting differences on the New York and American stock exchanges by examining the reaction to non-US company earnings announcements and 20-K (now 20-F) filings. Specifically, Meek tested whether either or both reporting events were associated with abnormal share returns. The results showed that earnings announcements for non-US firms based on domestic accounting principles caused a market reaction, but the release of the US reconciliation data was not considered an important event. Furthermore, the reaction to the announcements of non-US companies was comparable to the reaction to a sample of US firms reporting under US GAAP. These results imply that US investors can overcome the lack of comparability of financial statements, as they do not appear to wait until the reconciliation data are released by the SEC to react to the foreign accounting information. Therefore, even though profit figures are reported under foreign accounting principles, investors still regard this information as useful.

In a more recent study, however, Rees (1995) found that the market does react to Form 20-F disclosures, implying that the reconciliations to US GAAP do provide information to the market when 20-F is filed. Similarly, Pope and Rees (1992) found that US GAAP earnings adjustments add marginal explanatory power to a returns/earnings model, also consistent with investors and analysts using the US profits reconciliations.

There is also evidence that accounting information prepared using US standards may be as useful to home investors as their domestic accounting information. Etter (1998) discovered that Japanese investors found information content in the US GAAP consolidated earnings announcements released by Japanese companies, although this was based on a relatively small sample of 18 companies.

In the first study of the value relevance of overseas accounting data, Amir *et al.* (1993) compared US versus non-US GAAP accounting measures for 20 countries. Share returns were regressed on levels and changes in domestic earnings and US GAAP reconciliations as illustrated below:

$$R_{jt} = \alpha_0 + \alpha_1 \frac{E^F_{jt}}{P^F_{jt-1}} + \alpha_2 \frac{\Delta E^F_{jt}}{P^F_{jt-1}} + \alpha_{31} \frac{DE_{jt}}{P^F_{jt-1}} + \alpha_{32} \frac{\Delta DE_{jt}}{P^F_{jt-1}} + \varepsilon_{jt}$$

where R_{jt} represents 15 month returns for firm j at time t, P represents firm share price, E^F represents annual foreign (i.e., non-US) profits for the same firm, ΔE^F represents changes in foreign earnings and DE and ΔDE represent US GAAP reconciliations and changes in reconciliations respectively. If foreign accounting data are useful to investors in the US, the estimated coefficients on these variables (i.e., α_1 and/or α_2) will be significantly different from zero. If the reconciliations to US GAAP are value relevant, (that is, US investors only consider their accounting principles useful) then the relevant coefficients in the model (α_{31} and/or α_{32}) will be non-zero.[7]

Amir *et al.* (1993) found that the coefficients on both profits and changes in profits based on foreign accounting principles were significantly different from zero, indicating that US investors do use foreign accounting data in setting share prices. However, there was mixed evidence of the value relevance of the reconciliations. The absolute level of the reconciliation of foreign accounting information to US GAAP was useful, but the change in the reconciliation was not.[8] This research therefore suggests that foreign accounting data are useful to US investors in determining share prices of non-US companies, although US investors also find the reconciliations to familiar accounting principles useful, i.e., US investors perceive US-based reported figures to add incremental information to foreign reported figures.

In a comparative study of UK, Australian and Canadian companies, Barth and Clinch (1996) investigated whether differences between domestic accounting principles and US GAAP were used by investors in setting share prices. Specific accounting differences including goodwill, deferred tax and foreign currency were investigated using similar model specifications to Amir *et al.* (1993). Barth and Clinch found that domestic (i.e., non-US) accounting information (profits and changes in profits) is correlated with share returns for UK and Australian firms, indicating that investors use the 20-F reconciliations in setting share prices for UK and Australian firms. For Canadian firms, however, reconciliations to US GAAP provided no incremental explanatory power.

In respect of the individual reconciling items, Barth and Clinch found that adjustments to US GAAP for goodwill and intangibles were useful to investors for UK and Australian companies. Specifically, the results suggested that goodwill amortisation expenses were too low under UK and Australian accounting principles. Interestingly, in tests which split adjustments to US GAAP into positive and negative adjustments, Barth and Clinch found that for UK firms only negative differences were significantly related to share prices. This indicates that investors are more concerned about differences which result in UK income being higher than US income.

In contrast to these results, which generally indicate that US-based accounting data on foreign companies are useful to US investors, Chan and Seow (1996) provide evidence suggesting that the original domestic accounting data are more relevant to US investors than those reconciled to

[7] Amir *et al.* (1993) also regressed market to book ratios upon book value, earnings and reconciliations to assess the value of shareholders' equity reconciliations.

[8] Their results for market to book values indicated that shareholders' equity reconciliations are also value relevant.

US GAAP. They propose that this is attributable to diversity across business environments being untranslatable, resulting in the translation to US GAAP actually losing information.

In the most recent study of this issue, Fulkerson and Meek (1998) suggest that the reason that the evidence on the usefulness of 20-F reconciliation data is inconclusive is because analysts may pre-empt these announcements. They argue that analysts forecast earnings before the release of the reconciliation data, thus pre-empting the information in the reconciliations. Fulkerson and Meek's results confirm their hypothesis. When the sample was split into three groups (UK influence, Continental European influence and Other Country) they found that analysts appeared to pre-empt the information for the UK influence group, but the reconciliation appeared to be useful to analysts of European companies (the results of the 'other' group were not significant). Hence, US GAAP reconciliations for companies from countries with accounting systems unlike the US are particularly useful to analysts, while analysts from countries such as the UK are able to pre-empt the 20-F and use their own interpretative skills to discern the relevant information.

Market-based research into the usefulness of foreign accounting data therefore indicates that such information is relevant to investors in their share price decisions, even though it is based on different accounting standards. Foreign profits figures have consistently been found to be useful to investors when determining share prices. The evidence on the usefulness of SEC reconciliation data, however, is less conclusive. The results appear to be sensitive to model specification and/or the data and time period analysed. Given the significance of the debate on whether the SEC should be imposing costs on foreign companies (and consequently deterring many companies from listing on US exchanges), the issue of whether investors find US GAAP information useful is clearly important and worthy of future research.

5.6 SUMMARY

This chapter has reviewed the research into the information used in analysis of domestic and foreign equities by institutional investors and analysts. The annual report, financial statement information and direct management contact represent the most important and most useful sources to analysts and fund managers, although historical analysis shows a shift in the relative importance of these sources over time. While earlier studies showed that the annual report was the most useful source, recent research demonstrates that contact with company management is now the most heavily used.

In a domestic context, the financial statements are an essential part of the decision-making process, even though they are often criticised for containing only historical information. The profit and loss account forms an integral part of the appraisal techniques used by analysts and fund managers; this result holds over time and across countries.

Compared to the wealth of research into the information sources used in domestic analysis, the information used to analyse overseas shares has received little research attention. In general, accounting information based on local accounting principles appears to be useful in transnational investment decisions. However, the findings of research into the usefulness of reconciled (US GAAP) accounting information are inconclusive. There is also limited evidence to suggest that investors and analysts appear to view harmonisation positively.

What is unclear is the effect of international accounting differences and the means by which analysts and investors cope with these differences. For example, is foreign accounting information supplemented or augmented by other information sources? Do international accounting differences represent a material impediment to effective transnational decision making? Are alternative analysis techniques used to mitigate reliance on non-comparable accounting data? Such questions form the basis for the remainder of the book. The following chapter outlines the research methods used in the empirical study. This is then followed by three chapters that present the empirical results.

5.7 REFERENCES

Amir, E., Harris, T.S. and Venuti, E.K. (1993). 'A comparison of the value relevance of US versus non-US GAAP accounting measures using Form 20-F reconciliations.' *Journal of Accounting Research*, **31**, Supplement, 230–264.

Anderson, R. (1981). 'The usefulness of other information disclosed in corporate annual reports to institutional investors in Australia.' *Accounting and Business Research*, **Autumn**, 259–265.

Arnold, J. and Moizer, P. (1984). 'A survey of the methods used by UK investment analysts to appraise investments in ordinary shares.' *Accounting and Business Research*, **Summer**, 195–207.

Arnold, J., Moizer, P. and Noreen, E. (1984). 'Investment appraisal methods of financial analysts: A comparative study of US and UK practices.' *International Journal of Accounting*, **Spring**, 1–18.

Ball, R. and Kothari, S.P. (1991). 'Security returns around earnings announcements.' *The Accounting Review*, **66** (4), 718–738.

Barker, R.G. (1998). 'The market for information: evidence from finance directors, analysts and fund managers.' *Accounting and Business Research*, **29** (1), 1–20.

Barker, R. (1999). 'Survey and market-based evidence of industry-dependence in analysts' preferences between the dividend yield and price-earnings ratio valuation models.' *Journal of Business Finance and Accounting*, **26** (3), 393–418.

Barth, M.E. and Clinch, G. (1996). 'International accounting differences and their relation to share prices: evidence from UK, Australian and Canadian Firms.' *Contemporary Accounting Research*, **13** (1), 135–170.

Beattie, V.A. (2000). 'The future of business reporting: a review article.' *Irish Accounting Review*, **7** (1), 1–36.

Bence, D., Hapeshi, K. and Hussey, R. (1995). 'Examining investment information sources for sophisticated investors using cluster analysis.' *Accounting and Business Research*, **26** (1), 19–26.

Bhushan, R. and Lessard, D.R. (1992). 'Coping with international accounting diversity: fund managers' views on disclosure, reconciliation, and harmonization.' *Journal of International Financial Management and Accounting*, **4** (2), 149–164.

Breton, G. and Taffler, R.J. (1995). 'Creative accounting and investment analyst response.' *Accounting and Business Research*, **Spring**, 81–92.

Chan, K.C. and Seow, G.S. (1996). 'The association between stock returns and foreign GAAP earnings versus earnings adjusted to US GAAP.' *Journal of Accounting and Economics*, **21**, 139–158.

Choi, F.D.S. and Levich, R.M. (1991). 'Behavioral effects of international accounting diversity.' *Accounting Horizons*, **June**, 1–13.

Day, J.F.S. (1986). 'The use of annual reports by UK investment analysts.' *Accounting and Business Research*, **Autumn**, 295–307.

Etter, E.R. (1998). 'The information content of U.S. versus Japanese GAAP annual and quarterly earnings announcements and their relative informativeness to Japanese investors: a small sample case study.' *Journal of International Accounting, Auditing & Taxation*, **7** (2), 233–249.

Fulkerson, C.L. and Meek, G.K. (1998). 'Analysts' earnings forecasts and the value relevance of 20-F reconciliations from non-US to US GAAP.' *Journal of International Financial Management and Accounting*, **9** (1), 1–15.

Gniewosz, G. (1990). 'The share investment decision process and information use: an exploratory case study.' *Accounting and Business Research*, **20** (79), 223–230.

Govindarajan, V. (1980). 'The objectives of financial statements: an empirical study of the use of cash flow and earnings by security analysts.' *Accounting, Organisations and Society*, **5** (4), 383–392.

Hand, J.R.M. (1990). 'A test of the extended functional fixation hypothesis.' *The Accounting Review*, **65** (4), 740–763.

Hand, J.R.M. (1991). 'Extended functional fixation and security returns around earnings announcements: a reply to ball and kothari.' *The Accounting Review*, **66** (4), 739–746.

Hines, R.D. (1982). 'The usefulness of annual reports: the anomaly between the efficient markets hypothesis and shareholder surveys.' *Accounting and Business Research*, **Autumn**, 296–309.

Holland, J. (1998). 'Private disclosure and financial reporting.' *Accounting and Business Research*, **28** (4), 255–269.

Hopwood, A.G. (1994). 'Some reflections on "The Harmonization of Accounting Within the EU".' *The European Accounting Review*, **3** (2), 241–253.

Lee, T.A. and Tweedie, D.P. (1981). *The Institutional Investor and Financial Information*. The Institute of Chartered Accountants in England and Wales, London.

Lundholm, R.J. (1995). 'A tutorial on the Ohlson and Feltham/Ohlson models: answers to some frequently asked questions.' *Contemporary Accounting Research*, **11** (2), 749–761.

Marston, C. (1993). 'Company communications with analysts and fund managers. A study of the investor relations activities of large UK quoted companies.' Unpublished Ph.D. Thesis, Glasgow University.

Marston, C. (1999). *Investor Relations Meetings: Views of Companies, Institutional Investors and Analysts*, Institute of Chartered Accountants of Scotland, Edinburgh.

Marton, J. (1998). *Accounting and Stock Markets: A Study of Swedish Accounting for International Investors and Analysts*, BAS, Gothenburg University, Sweden.

Meek, G.K. (1983). 'U.S. securities market responses to alternate earnings disclosures of non-U.S. multinational corporations.' *The Accounting Review*, **58** (2), 394–402.

Miles, S. and Nobes, C. (1998). 'The use of foreign accounting data in UK financial institutions.' *Journal of Business Finance and Accounting*, **25** (3 and 4), 309–328.

Moizer, P. and Arnold, J. (1984). 'Share appraisal by investment analysts – portfolio vs. non-portfolio managers.' *Accounting and Business Research*, **Autumn**, 341–348.

Ohlson, J. (1989). 'Accounting earnings, book value, and dividends: the theory of the clean surplus equation,' (Part I), Unpublished Paper, Columbia University.

Ohlson, J. (1990). 'A synthesis of security theory and the role of dividends, cash flows and earnings.' *Contemporary Accounting Research*, **Spring**, 648–676.

Ohlson, J. (1991). 'The theory of value and earnings and an introduction to the Ball and Brown analysis.' *Contemporary Accounting Research*, **Fall**, 1–19.

Olbert, L. (1994). 'Stock valuation methods of financial analysts in a thin stock market in Sweden, with comparisons to the United Kingdom and the United States.' *International Journal of Accounting*, **29**, 123–135.

Peasnell, K. (1982). Some formal connections between economic values and yields and accounting numbers.' *Journal of Business Finance and Accounting*, **9** (3), 361–381.

Penman, S. (1992). 'Return to fundamentals.' *Journal of Accounting, Auditing and Finance*, **7**, 465–483.

Pike, R., Meerjanssen, J. and Chadwick, L. (1993). 'The appraisal of ordinary shares by investment analysts in the UK and Germany.' *Accounting and Business Research*, **23** (92), 489–499.

Pope, P.F. and Rees, W.P. (1992). 'International differences in GAAP and the pricing of earnings.' *Journal of International Financial Management and Accounting*, **4** (33), 190–219.

Preinreich, G. (1938). 'Annual survey of economic theory: the theory of depreciation.' *Econometrica*, **6** (3), 219–241.

Previts, G.J., Bricker, R.J., Robinson, T.R. and Young, S.J. (1994). 'A content analysis of sell-side analyst company reports.' *Accounting Horizons*, **8** (2), 55–70.

Rees, L. (1995). 'The information contained in reconciliations to earnings based on US accounting principles by non-US Companies.' *Accounting and Business Research*, **25** (100), 301–310.

Shleifer, A. (2000) *Inefficient Markets: An Introduction to Behavioral Finance*. Oxford University Press, Oxford.

Tinic, S.M. (1990). 'A perspective on the stock market's fixation on accounting numbers.' *The Accounting Review*, **65** (4), 781–796.

Vergoossen, R. (1993). 'The use and perceived importance of annual reports by investment analysts in the Netherlands.' *The European Accounting Review*, **2**, 219–244.

6

Methodology

6.1 INTRODUCTION

As the previous chapters demonstrate, there are many ways of investigating how useful various information sources and appraisal techniques are to analysts and fund managers. Most common are survey methods, particularly questionnaires and interviews, which are the two methods employed in the current study. This chapter assesses the strengths and weaknesses of questionnaires and interviews and discusses why both were used. The chapter provides details of the response rates from the questionnaire and then outlines how the questionnaire and interview data were analysed.

6.2 DATA COLLECTION

6.2.1 The questionnaire survey

6.2.1.1 Strengths and weaknesses of questionnaires

By far the most popular method used in previous research into the information sources and techniques used by investment analysts and institutional investors is the questionnaire. Questionnaires are useful for gaining an overall picture of a research issue, especially where the theory in the relevant area is not well developed. Relative to other qualitative methods such as interviews, questionnaires require less time to complete, code and analyse and are generally less expensive to administer. This enables large samples to be taken, and may therefore permit generalisation of the results to the population.

One of the most common problems with questionnaire surveys is the risk of low response rates. Low response rates are particularly common when surveying the investment community as, in addition to the time pressures faced by potential respondents, some firms prevent their employees from responding to questionnaires (Schipper, 1991). This may lead to biased results if respondents and non-respondents have materially different views. However, a number of solutions are available to deal with non-response bias. One of the most popular measures is to treat late respondents as non-respondents, as recommended by Oppenheim (1992). Statistical tests can then be conducted on the two samples of early and late respondents in order to see if they differ significantly.

6.2.1.2 Questionnaire used in the current research

The questionnaire used in the current study was designed with reference to previous research into the use of information in equity decisions in a domestic context, but modified to take into account potential differences in transnational decisions. During the design stage of the questionnaire, numerous listed company annual reports from various countries were examined in order to check for any significant international variation in terminology and format. Any differences (although there were few) were then accommodated in the phrases used in the questions on the individual sections of the questionnaire. The annual reports surveyed were mainly English language versions and the general format of the reports was similar. This does imply a size bias towards larger, more international companies, but it was assumed that analysts and investors would be primarily involved with these companies. For example, prior research has demonstrated a clear, positive association between investment analyst following and firm size, (e.g., Lang and Lundholm, 1996).

The questionnaire consisted of seven sections, comprising a mixture of open ended and closed questions. The majority were closed questions on an ordinal scale of 1 to 5. Two open-ended questions were also included in order to provide an opportunity for the respondents to add any relevant comments.

Section one of the questionnaire related to the background characteristics of respondents' employment and was designed to obtain information on analysts of UK and foreign companies. Respondents were asked to indicate whether they were fund managers or analysts, whether or not they were industry specialists, and, if so, which industries they specialised in.

The second section consisted of a number of questions relevant only to analysts of foreign companies. Analysts solely of UK companies were therefore requested not to complete this section. Respondents were asked which version of the annual report they used, the impact of accounting differences on their decisions and their views on the harmonisation of international accounting standards.

One of the difficulties of collecting data for this research was the possibility of differences between the analysis techniques of analysts of companies from different countries or geographic regions. To classify analysts solely on the basis of whether they analyse UK or foreign companies risks over-simplification. Analysis techniques and information sources of analysts of foreign companies may vary according to the companies' country of domicile. A number of questions in section 2 and in subsequent sections of the questionnaire were consequently designed to allow the importance of information sources and appraisal techniques to vary for the same respondent between different countries.

From section three onwards, the questionnaire was designed for respondents who analyse UK companies and for analysts of foreign companies. Section three related to the analysis techniques used by analysts and fund managers. Respondents were requested to rate, on a scale of 1 to 5, various analysis techniques shown to be important in prior research. Section four covered the sources of information used in their analysis (i.e., the perceived usefulness of the sources, and the frequency of use). Section five related specifically to the different sections of the annual report and section six contained biographical questions. In order to permit respondents to remain anonymous, section 6 was optional. Finally, section seven contained two open-ended questions relating to the perceived costs of international accounting differences, and any information not covered in the questionnaire that the respondents felt was important.

Before the main survey was conducted, the questionnaire was circulated for comments to colleagues (one of whom was a former employee in an investor relations department of a large UK listed plc), other academic researchers in the field and an investment analyst working for a UK stockbroker. A pilot study was then conducted, with questionnaires being sent to 100 members of the Institute of Investment Management and Research (IIMR).[1] Twenty-five responses were received and no material changes were recommended, with the exception of the addition of two frequently used analysis techniques: economic value added (EVA) analysis, and a subjective assessment of management. Although the latter is perhaps more strictly a subset of an analysis technique, its omission was observed by a number of respondents in the pilot study and therefore included in the final version.

The final version of the questionnaire was sent to all Associate Members and Fellows of the IIMR after a list of members' names and addresses was kindly supplied by the Institute. In total, 1980 questionnaires were distributed in January 1999. Due to the typically low response rates received from such surveys, the maximum possible number of questionnaires was sent. After the initial mailing, a second batch of questionnaires was mailed to facilitate tests for non-response bias. The second version of the questionnaire contained questions on respondents' background characteristics, and views of harmonisation and international accounting diversity; however, questions on the usefulness of appraisal techniques and information sources were not included.

[1] The IIMR has since become the UK Society of Investment Professionals (UKSIP).

Table 6.1 Response rates to the questionnaire survey

	Initial mailing		Follow-up		Total	
	No.	%	No.	%	No.	%
UK analysis only	137	42	88	44	225	43
Foreign analysis†	103	32	52	26	155	30
Non-usable	86	26	59	30	145	28
Total	326	100	199	100	525	100

† Includes analysts and fund managers involved in both UK and foreign company analysis.

6.2.1.3 Response rates

In total, 525 responses were received, resulting in a response rate of 27%. Of the total number of questionnaires received, 145 responses were unusable: the final usable response rate was, therefore, 19%. Table 6.1 provides details of the responses from the two mailings.[2] The high number of non-usable responses was mainly attributable to the fact that the list of IIMR members contained non-active members and analysts of bonds and other debt securities. Only active fund managers and analysts were selected. Analysts of fixed income securities were excluded because the information needs of credit analysts differ from the needs of equity analysts, and are outside the scope of this research.

The usable response rate of 19% is comparable with response rates obtained in recent studies. Carter and Van Auken (1990) attained a response rate of 20% in a survey of US based analysts, while in a questionnaire survey that involved Hong Kong-based analysts and fund managers, Wong and Cheung (1999) attained a response rate of 14%.

6.2.1.4 Tests for non-response bias

In order to ascertain whether non-response bias was a problem with the questionnaire data, tests for differences between early and late respondents were conducted. No significant differences were found between the number of companies analysed or the experience of the early and late respondents. The two groups did not differ significantly in their views on the harmonisation, or the impact of international accounting differences on their decision making. Non-response bias does not, therefore, appear to be a substantial

[2] The sections on the usefulness of appraisal techniques and information sources were based on the responses to the first mailing.

problem according to these tests. However, this is only a proxy for the extent of non-response bias, and the response rate of 19% must be borne in mind when interpreting the findings.

6.2.2 Semi-structured interviews

6.2.2.1 Strengths and weaknesses of interviews

Interviews have become increasingly common in research into equity analysis by analysts and institutional investors in recent years (e.g., Barker, 1998; Marton, 1998; Marston, 1999). Interviews have a number of key advantages over other more quantitative research methods such as questionnaires and market-based research. For example, Guba and Lincoln (1994, p. 106) point out that 'precise quantitative approaches that focus on selected subsets of variables necessarily "strip" from consideration, through appropriate controls or randomization, other variables that exist in the context that might, if allowed to exert their effects, greatly alter findings'. Respondents are able to express detailed answers to questions, and opportunities arise which enable the respondent to clarify the interview questions and also permit the interviewer to clarify potentially ambiguous responses.

Compared to other data collection methods, the significant disincentives to using interviews are the expense incurred in travel costs, the time spent in the collection of the data, and the amount of time required by the researcher to process and interpret the data. Thus, while interviews enable a more comprehensive view to be obtained, the data which facilitate this are often difficult to analyse and portray in a succinct, yet comprehensive manner. Due to the time required by the participant, gaining access may also be problematic when conducting interviews. Questionnaires can be quicker to complete than interviews and can be completed in the respondents' own time. Interviews, however, may be lengthy and require significant time commitments. These factors represent the research costs of collecting a rich data set and can impose significant constraints on the number of responses. A corollary of this is that the results of the research are not as generalisable as the data collected from large samples by questionnaires or market-based methods.

Although subjectivity in the interpretation of the data may militate against the advantages of interviews (e.g., Barker, 1998 p. 6), steps can be taken to reduce such bias. A useful method is the approach recommended by Patton (1990) and Miles and Huberman (1994). This involves using the interview schedule to guide the work as a descriptive framework for analysis. Thus, a structure is imposed for the data analysis which reduces the scope for subjectivity in the interpretation of responses.

6.2.2.2 Interviews used in the current research

Semi-structured, formal interviews were conducted with fund managers and analysts involved in the analysis of foreign equities, with a view to elaboration on specific important or interesting results from the questionnaire survey and to investigate additional related issues in more depth. Section seven of the questionnaire contained a place for respondents to indicate whether they would participate in a follow-up interview. All 42 analysts and fund managers of foreign companies who agreed to participate were then contacted to arrange an appointment. Thirty-one interviews were finally conducted during the period November 1999 to March 2000.[3] The remaining 11 had either left their organisation since completing the questionnaire and left no contact address, or due to changes in circumstances, were unable to participate.

An interview schedule that contained nine sections was used; each section contained a list of open-ended questions. The questions were divided into the following sections:

(i) the background of the respondent and the company;
(ii) the results of the questionnaire survey;
(iii) fund managers' and analysts' decision-making processes;
(iv) the role of accounting and other information in the analysis process;
(v) the perceived quality of accounting information from different countries;
(vi) views on the harmonisation of accounting standards;
(vii) the role of intermediaries in the analysis process;
(viii) company meetings and visits;
(ix) any other issues not addressed.

Although the schedule provided an overarching framework for the interview and ensured that the sequence of questions asked was consistent, sufficient flexibility was allowed to permit follow up and supplementary questions if any of the responses were unclear or worthy of further investigation. With the exception of two respondents and the telephone interviews, the interviews were recorded, the tapes transcribed verbatim, and the transcriptions checked to the original tapes.

In common with a number of studies into equity analysis techniques, (e.g., Arnold and Moizer, 1984; Barker, 1998) multiple research designs were used in order to ameliorate potential problems arising from the limitations of individual research methods in an attempt to 'triangulate' across

[3] Two interviews were conducted over the telephone due to respondents' time constraints. The remainder were conducted at the respondents' organisations.

methods. This enables different perspectives to be taken on the same research problem. As Jick (1979, p. 602) explains: 'organizational researchers can improve the accuracy of their judgements by collecting different kinds of data bearing on the same phenomenon'. Rather than perceiving quantitative and qualitative methods as competing, triangulation views them as complementary, recognising that each can enrich and validate the other.

6.3 ANALYSIS OF THE DATA

6.3.1 Questionnaire data

The data collected in the current research require both parametric and non-parametric testing. Parametric tests should only be used when a number of conditions are satisfied. First, data must be measured on at least an interval scale. Second, the samples should be drawn from populations which are normally distributed and homoskedastic, i.e., have equal variances. The importance of these conditions has, however, been questioned by a number of authors (e.g., Boneau, 1960). The specific tests used are described and discussed below.

6.3.1.1 T-tests

For data measured on an interval or ratio sale, differences between two means can be tested for statistical significance using the t-test. Assuming normally distributed populations, random samples and equivalent 'within group' variances, the t-test tests the null of equivalence of population means, formally stated:

$$\mathrm{H}_0 : \mu_\mathrm{A} - \mu_\mathrm{B} = 0$$

where H_0 is the null hypothesis, and μ_A, μ_B are the population means for the two groups.

The t-test is conducted by first assessing the variability within the two groups, and then expressing the difference between the two group means as a proportion of the average within-group-difference.

6.3.1.2 Mann-Whitney U test

The Mann-Whitney *U* test can broadly be described as the non-parametric equivalent of the t-test as it is used to test whether two independent groups have been drawn from the same population. Although the *U*-test is a powerful test (Siegel, 1956) it does not have the same restrictive assumptions underpinning it as the t-test (i.e., of normality and equality of variance). Therefore, it only requires ordinal data, rather than interval data. The Mann-Whitney *U* test was therefore used to test whether there were significant differences between two samples in the responses to the questions on the 5 point scale.

6.3.1.3 Kruskal-Wallis

The Kruskal-Wallis test is designed to test whether *k* independent samples are from different populations and like the Mann-Whitney *U* test, only requires ordinal data. The Kruskal-Wallis test is based upon a comparison of the sum of ranks of observations where the samples are combined and ranked in a single series. The test then 'determines whether these sums of ranks are so disparate that they are not likely to have come from samples which were all drawn from the same population' (Siegel, 1956, p. 185). The Kruskal-Wallis test was used on questionnaire data to test for differences in the average response to questions on a 5 point scale between more than two samples.

6.3.1.4 Chi-Squared test

The chi-squared test is used to test for association between variables that are measured on a nominal scale. The test is commonly used in the social sciences and uses a contingency table, where observed outcomes are compared with expected outcomes. Where no association exists, the expected values should approximate or equal the observed values. The chi-squared test is given by:

$$\chi^2 = \sum \frac{(O_i - E_i)^2}{E_i}$$

where O_i represents observed values, while E_i represents expected values. Thus, the chi-squared statistic increases with the differences between observed and expected values. The hypothesis of independence is therefore rejected for large values of χ^2 because the observed values differ substantially to their expected values. Specifically, the null hypothesis of independence can be rejected where χ^2 exceeds a critical value for a given level of significance and for a given number of degrees of freedom (given by $(r - 1)(c - 1)$, where r = the number of rows and c = number of columns in the contingency table).

6.3.2 Analysis of the interview data

The analysis of the interview data was based on the approach advocated by Miles and Huberman (1994) which relies upon matrices as a framework for the distillation, analysis, and summarisation of qualitative data. Miles and Huberman identify two approaches to analysing interview data. The first approach is case-orientated, where cases are taken as the unit of analysis, i.e., the specific characteristics of the individual or group under study are preserved throughout the analysis. The second approach is variable-orientated. This is where the focus of analysis is upon specific variables or themes, which are compared and contrasted in order to identify any potential relationships between them. The variable-orientated analysis transcends specific cases, so individual case details are concealed and eventually ignored.

Both case-orientated and variable-orientated approaches have considerable advantages. By maintaining details of the individual cases a more complex analysis can be conducted and specific details can be drawn out. However, the cost of this is that the findings remain particular to individual cases and may not apply to others. The variable orientated approach is better able to identify themes and patterns, but is less able to tackle complexities of causation. Miles and Huberman (1994) therefore advocate a combination of the two strategies rather than strict adherence to one. Accordingly, the approach used in the current study involved a synthesis of both variable and case-orientated analysis. This enabled a greater degree of generalisability than the case orientated approach *per se*. It also preserved valuable narrative excerpts which are useful for exemplifying patterns and findings.

6.4 SUMMARY

This chapter has outlined the research approach used in the following research study. A two-stage methodology was adopted. The first stage involved a questionnaire sent to members of the Institute of Investment Management and Research (IIMR). A response rate broadly in line with previous similar studies was attained. In the second stage and, in order to elucidate further the findings of the questionnaire and to explore further issues in more depth, 31 interviews were conducted with investment analysts and fund managers involved in investment in foreign equities. While the questionnaire survey facilitated statistical testing of the results, the interviews permitted detailed responses to questions and provided a valuable insight into transnational decision making. The following chapters present and discuss the data collected from both the questionnaire survey and the interviews.

6.5 REFERENCES

Arnold, J. and Moizer, P. (1984). 'A survey of the methods used by UK investment analysts to appraise investments in ordinary shares.' *Accounting and Business Research*, **Summer**, 195–207.

Barker, R.G. (1998). 'The market for information: evidence from finance directors, analysts and fund managers.' *Accounting and Business Research*, **29** (1), 1–20.

Boneau, C. A. (1960). 'The effects of violations of assumptions underlying the t test.' *Psychological Bulletin*, **57**, 49–64.

Carter, R.B. and Van Auken, H.E. (1990). 'Security analysis and portfolio management: a survey and analysis.' *Journal of Portfolio Management*, **Spring**, 81–85.

Guba, E.G. and Lincoln, Y.S. (1994). 'Competing paradigms in qualitative research.' In *Handbook of Qualitative Research*, Norman K. Denzin and Yvonna S. Lincoln, eds. Sage Publications, Thousand Oaks, California.

Jick, T.D. (1979). 'Mixing qualitative and quantitative methods: triangulation in action.' *Administrative Science Quarterly*, **24**, 602–611.

Lang, M.H. and Lundholm, R.J. (1996). 'Corporate disclosure policy and analyst behaviour.' *The Accounting Review*, **71** (4), 467–492.

Marston, C. (1999). *Investor Relations Meetings: Views of Companies, Institutional Investors and Analysts*, Institute of Chartered Accountants of Scotland, Edinburgh.

Marton, J. (1998). *Accounting and Stock Markets: A Study of Swedish Accounting for International Investors and Analysts*, BAS, Gothenburg University, Sweden.

Miles, M.B. and Huberman, A.M. (1994). *Qualitative Data Analysis*, 2nd edn, Sage Publications, Thousand Oaks, California.

Oppenheim, A.N. (1992). *Questionnaire Design and Attitude Measurement*, 2nd edn, St. Martin's Press, New York.

Patton, M.Q. (1990). *Qualitative Evaluation and Research Methods*, 2nd edn, Sage, London.

Schipper, K. (1991). 'Analysts' forecasts.' *Accounting Horizons*, **December**, 105–121.

Siegel, S. (1956). *Nonparametric Statistics for the Behavioural Sciences*. McGraw-Hill, New York.

Wong, M.C. and Cheung, Y.L. (1999). 'The practice of investment management in Hong Kong: market forecasting and stock selection.' *OMEGA*, **27**, 451–465.

7 Transnational Equity Appraisal Techniques

7.1 INTRODUCTION

Chapter 3 demonstrated that international differences in financial reporting can be material, both in terms of the quality of measurement of accounting numbers, and in terms of the quality of the overall financial disclosure. Moreover, and as outlined in Chapter 4, there has been very little research to date into how the presence of national boundaries affects equity investment decisions. This chapter presents the results of the empirical research into the techniques used by analysts and fund managers in the analysis of domestic (UK) and overseas equities. Following a description of the sample, interview and questionnaire data are presented in order to ascertain whether fundamental analysis is as important in analysing overseas equities as it is in a domestic context. In addition to this, the chapter evaluates the importance of the various other appraisal techniques available to analysts and fund managers. Finally, the chapter discusses whether, when analysing foreign companies, investors and analysts adapt the fundamental approach to make allowances for differences in the information environment.

7.2 BACKGROUND OF RESPONDENTS

7.2.1 Sample composition

Table 7.1 shows the breakdown of the sample between investment analysts and fund managers involved in domestic (i.e., UK company) and transnational (i.e., overseas company) analysis.[1] The sample is split relatively evenly between those involved in domestic and transnational analysis (59% domestic versus 41% transnational). However, the majority of the sample for both domestic and transnational analysis is represented by fund managers, rather than investment analysts. This is consistent with the

[1] In accordance with Moizer and Arnold (1984), this classification is based on whether or not the respondent is responsible for a portfolio. Thus, buy-side analysts and sell-side analysts are included in the 'analyst' category. Results based on a classification of sell-side versus buy-side analysts yielded very similar results.

Table 7.1 Sample description

	Fund managers		Investment analysts		Total	
	No.	%	No.	%	No.	%
Domestic analysis	152	67.6	73	32.4	225	59.2
Transnational analysis†	108	69.7	47	30.3	155	40.8
Total	260	68.4	120	31.6	380	100

† Throughout the book, the category of analysts of foreign companies (referred to as the 'transnational analysis' category) includes fund managers and investment analysts who analyse both UK and foreign companies.

findings of Weetman *et al.* (1994), who note a shift in balance in the investment industry towards the buy-side.

Details of the activity of the employers of analysts of UK companies and foreign companies are provided in Table 7.2. Unsurprisingly, investment management firms employ the greatest number of respondents (almost half of the sample) in both domestic and transnational categories. Stockbrokers, insurance firms and investment banks are the next most popular categories, together employing 36%. Respondents in the 'other' category worked in the public sector, charities, consultancy firms and in private finance/research.

7.2.2 Number of companies analysed

Table 7.3 shows the number of companies analysed by analysts and fund managers who follow domestic and foreign companies. The table reveals that the means are very similar for the two groups (which comprise both

Table 7.2 Employers of analysts and fund managers

	Domestic analysis		Transnational analysis		Total	
Type of organisation	No.	%	No.	%	No.	%
Investment management	114	50.6	72	46.5	186	49.0
Stockbroker	41	18.2	17	11.0	58	15.3
Insurance company	23	10.2	20	12.9	43	11.3
Investment bank	14	6.2	22	14.2	36	9.5
Pension fund	17	7.6	11	7.1	28	7.4
Commercial bank	5	2.2	6	3.9	11	2.9
Other	11	4.9	7	4.5	18	4.7
Total	**225**	**100**	**155**	**100**	**380**	**100**

Table 7.3 Number of companies analysed

	Domestic analysis		Transnational analysis		Total	
Range (companies)	No.	%	No.	%	No.	%
0–25	35	18.3	31	21.5	66	19.7
25–50	51	26.7	26	18.1	77	23.0
51–75	10	5.2	11	7.6	21	6.3
76–100	37	19.4	27	18.8	64	19.1
101–125	5	2.6	3	2.1	8	2.4
126–150	14	7.3	11	7.6	25	7.5
Over 151	39	20.4	35	24.3	74	22.1
Total	**191**	**100**	**144**	**100**	**335**	**100**
Mean	114		118		116	
Median	75		100		80	
Standard deviation	130.37		114.60		123.67	

fund managers and investment analysts). A t-test revealed no significant differences between the average number of companies followed by analysts of domestic and overseas firms (t = 0.247; p = 0.805). The median number of companies analysed, however, indicates that analysts of foreign companies follow more companies than their domestic counterparts. This inconsistency between the mean and median is caused by a small number of very high values for fund management firms who adopt a quantitative approach to analysis and analyse a very high number of companies. These firms are also contributing to the large standard deviation of the number of companies analysed, which, for domestic analysts and for the overall sample, exceeds the mean.

When respondents are split into investment analysts and fund managers, as expected, and in line with prior research (e.g., Moizer and Arnold, 1984), clear differences emerge in respect of the number of companies analysed. Table 7.4 shows that, on average, fund managers analyse almost three times as many companies as investment analysts (145 versus 50). The medians for the two groups also confirm this disparity. A two-tailed t-test showed that the difference between the average number of companies analysed by fund managers and analysts is significant at the 0.01 level (t = 8.08; p = 0.000). The distribution of the number of companies analysed by investment analysts is also skewed towards fewer companies, with 77.7% analysing fewer than 50 companies. In contrast, only 27.1% of fund managers analysed fewer than 50 companies. Furthermore, over 70 fund managers (30.2%) analysed over 150 companies, whereas only four investment analysts (3.9%) covered such a high number.

Table 7.4 Number of companies analysed

	Fund managers		Investment analysts		Total	
Range (companies)	No.	%	No.	%	No.	%
0–25	20	8.6	46	44.7	66	19.7
25–50	43	18.5	34	33.0	77	23.0
51–75	15	6.5	6	5.8	21	6.3
76–100	55	23.7	9	8.7	64	19.1
101–125	5	2.2	3	2.9	8	2.4
126–150	24	10.3	1	1.0	25	7.5
Over 151	70	30.2	4	3.9	74	22.1
Total	**232**	**100**	**103**	**100**	**335**	**100**
Mean	145		50		116	
Median	100		30		80	
Standard deviation	132.02		49.85		123.67	

7.2.3 Countries analysed

The various countries analysed by fund managers and analysts is shown in Table 7.5. With the exception of the UK, the most popular countries for both fund managers and analysts are France and Germany.[2] An interesting finding is the relatively low coverage of the US, considering its economic significance. It is noteworthy that 31 fund managers (6.4%) and 19 analysts (7.7%) cover companies from the Netherlands, which had a GDP of $349.6 billion in 1999 (using average US$/Euro exchange rates from *Datastream*); in contrast, the US had a GDP of $9,299 billion in 1999, yet only 38 fund managers (7.8%) and 16 analysts (6.5%) analyse US companies.[3]

European countries thus clearly receive the most coverage. This concentration is confirmed by the cumulative percentage figures. The three most analysed countries (UK, France and Germany) represent over 60% of the total and, together, European countries represent over three quarters (77%) of the total. By contrast, the US and Japan together only receive 11.2% of the total. Nevertheless, these findings are in accordance with turnover in equities by country reported by the London Stock Exchange (2000). These figures show that France, Germany and Netherlands are respectively the countries with the highest turnover value in the year 2000 (excluding the UK). *Prima*

[2] Note that respondents were able to indicate all of the countries they covered; hence the difference between the number of times a country was covered (735 in total) and the total number of analysts and fund managers responding to this question (120 and 260 respectively).

[3] National income figures are taken from the International Montetary Fund (2000).

Table 7.5 Countries analysed by analysts and fund managers†

	Fund managers		Investment analysts		Total		
	No.	%	No.	%	No.	%	Cum %
United Kingdom	184	37.7	101	40.7	285	38.8	38.8
France	52	10.7	28	11.4	80	10.9	49.7
Germany	51	10.5	27	11.0	78	10.6	60.3
USA	38	7.8	16	6.5	54	7.3	67.6
Netherlands	31	6.4	19	7.7	50	6.8	74.4
Japan	24	4.9	5	2.0	29	3.9	78.3
Italy	13	2.7	8	3.3	21	2.9	81.2
Australia	13	2.7	6	2.4	19	2.6	83.8
Scandinavia	9	1.8	9	3.7	18	2.4	86.2
Hong Kong	12	2.5	5	2.0	17	2.3	88.5
Canada	11	2.3	2	0.8	13	1.8	90.3
Spain	10	2	3	1.2	13	1.8	92.1
Asia	11	2.3	1	0.4	12	1.6	93.7
Switzerland	5	1.0	6	2.4	11	1.5	95.2
Latin America	7	1.4	1	0.4	8	1.1	96.3
South Africa	4	0.8	2	0.8	6	0.8	97.1
Malaysia	5	1.0	0	0	5	0.7	97.8
Central Europe	2	0.4	2	0.8	4	0.5	98.3
Austria	0	0	2	0.8	2	0.3	98.6
Belgium	1	0.2	1	0.4	2	0.3	98.9
New Zealand	2	0.4	0	0	2	0.3	99.2
Portugal	1	0.2	1	0.4	2	0.3	99.5
Eastern Europe	0	0	1	0.4	1	0.1	99.6
Middle East	1	0.2	0	0	1	0.1	99.7
North Africa	1	0.2	0	0	1	0.1	99.8
Thailand	0	0	1	0.4	1	0.1	99.9
Total	**488**	**100**	**247**	**100**	**735**	**100**	**100**

† Based on responses from 260 fund managers and 120 investment analysts.

facie, at least, these results suggest that overall, geographic proximity is as much a determinant of country coverage as economic significance.

A further interesting point to note from Table 7.5 is that, with the exception of the US, the countries covered by investment analysts are concentrated around Europe and the UK. This contrasts with fund managers' coverage, which appears more widespread. For instance, 26.5% (129 out of 488) of the countries covered by fund managers are outside Europe compared to only 15.7% (39 out of 249) for investment analysts. Similarly, the numbers and proportions of fund managers covering companies in Asia and Australia

Table 7.6 Number of analysts specialising by country/region[†]

	Specialists	Non-specialists	Total	% specialists
Fund managers	47	61	108	43.5
Investment analysts	19	28	47	40.4
Total	**66**	**89**	**155**	**42.5**

[†] This only pertains to the 155 analysts and fund managers who analyse foreign companies.

are 65 and 13.4% respectively, whereas only 18 analysts (7.3%) analyse companies in this region. Based on this evidence, UK-based fund managers are less parochial than UK-based analysts.

7.2.4 Analyst and fund manager specialisation

The number and proportion of analysts involved in transnational analysis who specialise in companies from particular countries or geographic regions are shown in Table 7.6. A marginally higher proportion of fund managers specialise on a geographic basis, (43.5% versus 40.4% for investment analysts), although chi-squared tests revealed no significant difference between these proportions.

The breakdown of analysts and fund managers by domestic and foreign company analysis in Table 7.7, however, shows a different picture in respect of industry specialism. The proportion of investment analysts specialising by industry is substantially higher than the proportion of fund managers. This result holds for both UK and foreign company analysis.

Table 7.7 Number of analysts specialising by industry[†]

	Domestic analysis		Transnational analysis		Total	
	Specialist	Non-specialist	Specialist	Non-specialist	Specialist	% specialists
Fund managers	80	70	33	75	113	43.8
Investment analysts	50	23	33	14	83	69.2
Total	**130**	**93**	**66**	**89**	**196**	**51.9**

[†] Based on the responses from 260 fund managers and 120 investment analysts.

In total, the majority of fund managers do not specialise in the analysis of companies from specific industries or sectors (145 non-specialists versus 113 specialists). However, for both UK and foreign company investment analysts, the number of industry specialists is more than double the number of non-specialists (50 versus 23 and 33 versus 14 respectively).

As chi-squared tests on the figures in Table 7.7 revealed, the hypothesis of no relationship between fund managers and analysts was rejected at the 0.01 level for transnational analysis, and at the 0.05 level for domestic analysis. Investment analysts therefore specialise more by industry than fund managers. This is consistent with analysts generally possessing more detailed sector knowledge than fund managers. However, the results for geographic specialisation reveal few differences. Overall, the results indicate that sector specialism is more prevalent than geographic specialism in both groups.

In the interviews with analysts and fund managers, respondents were keen to emphasise that the ways in which analysts specialise have recently changed substantially. Whereas both groups have historically specialised in companies from particular countries, analysts and fund managers clearly felt that sector specialism has become more prevalent. This sector specialism generally applies to companies and sectors *within* certain geographic regions, so full global sector specialism has yet to be fully reached (as indicated by the results in the questionnaire survey). Analyst 2 provided an illustrative quote:[4]

> There is an increasing tendency to produce research on [a sectoral] basis, whereas if one goes back 10 years, it was organised more on country lines. [However] it is still important to take into account the country concept.

These changes appear to be partly driven by changes in sell-side analyst specialism, although they also appear to be influenced by the increasing number of global financial products offered by fund management firms. This in turn is a function of increasing numbers of global companies and industries. For example, Fund Manager 5 pointed out:

> Industry similarities are more important than national boundaries. For example, BP has more in common with large US oil companies than it has with those in the UK.

However, these changes are not affecting all industries to the same degree. For example, as noted by Analyst 1, oil companies and auto-manufacturers are considered global industries because the products are global. Retail and

[4] Numbers are attached to quotes from analysts and fund managers in order that the reader may refer to the Appendix, which provides more details on individual respondents.

construction, on the other hand, are delivered locally, and are therefore likely to require a degree of local specialist knowledge.

Although these changes are occurring globally, UK-based analysts and fund managers are particularly affected. They perceived London to be affected by additional forces towards sectors, rather than country-based specialism. Comments from both groups indicated that the number of UK analysts being involved *purely* in domestic analysis is waning, due to the increasing integration of European product and financial markets:

> If, for example, other [UK] analysts are looking at Ready Mix concrete, a company which makes more money in Germany than it does in the UK, obviously they need to know what is happening in Germany. (Analyst 1)

> In the short term, with specific reference to Europe, there is a trend towards running things on a pan-European basis, grouping UK and European assets together, and that tends to lead to more sector-based focus on a pan-European basis. Also, it is definitely the case that within particular industries, they are becoming more global in focus, so it is only natural that you are going to get more sector coverage in those circumstances. (Fund Manager 14)

However, Analyst 2 emphasised the need to keep country factors in mind; he also expressed reservations over the ability of UK analysts to cover European companies in sufficient depth:

> Everyone is trying to merge the UK with the rest of Europe, but the danger is you end up knowing a little about a great deal, rather than a great deal about a little.

As is the case with London and Europe, moves to sector specialism within a regional framework are taking place in other geographical areas, in line with the findings of the recent empirical research discussed in Chapter 2 which documents the increasing regionalisation of equity markets. This trend is reflected in the way both fund management firms and brokerage houses are organised. In particular, fund management firms in the sample were based around common regional divisions, i.e., Europe, Asia/Pacific (sometimes with Japan receiving specific attention), US and emerging markets. Therefore, with the possible exception of a small number of sectors, inter-regional barriers still appear to be significant enough to prevent truly global coverage.

As financial institutions shift from country specialism towards sectoral specialism, comparability of financial statements will become increasingly important, as international comparisons of financial and other company information will become more prevalent. However, to a degree, problems of comparability may be partly reduced by the fact that sector specialism still takes place within a regional framework.

7.2.4.1 Coverage of local versus secondary listed shares

As indicated in Chapter 2, the internationalisation of equity markets has, in part, been fuelled by companies listing their shares on overseas stock markets, with London playing host to the largest number of foreign firms of all other exchanges. However, what is unclear, is the degree to which analysts and fund managers confine themselves to investment in shares with a secondary listing. The interviewees were therefore asked about the extent to which they cover shares on the local versus the UK stock markets.[5]

All analysts and fund managers stated that they follow securities on the local stock market. This applies across various stock markets with significant variation in size, liquidity and stages of development (including, for example, US, South American, Japanese and Indian companies). Indeed, in the majority of cases, shares traded on the local market are prioritised relative to the UK market. However, a considerable number of analysts and fund managers (11 out of 30) deal with shares on the London market.[6]

The primary determinants of the market where shares are followed are price and liquidity. Fund Manager 8 noted that price anomalies rarely exist between markets, but quotes from fund managers indicate that differences between different markets can still influence the decision of where to trade. For example, Fund Managers 12 and 16 stated that they use the local market unless there is a valuation anomaly. In addition, Fund Manager 10 pointed out that he prefers local markets, as share prices for some emerging market equities trade at a premium in London, due to investment restrictions in the local market.

Such anomalies have important implications for the efficiency of international equity markets. In theory, provided that there are no differences in the nature of the securities between primary and secondary markets, any price differences should be immediately eliminated (at least to a level within transaction costs) via arbitrage. The results of the current research, however, are more in line with recent evidence of market inefficiency which demonstrates that identical assets do not necessarily trade at identical prices in different markets. In particular, Froot and Dabora (1999) find that movements in the prices of shares in Royal Dutch Shell, Unilever and SmithKline

[5] Throughout the remainder of this book, the term 'local' denotes the location of the company.

[6] The analysts and fund managers who cover US companies were an exception here, as they only followed shares on US markets.

Beecham vary substantially, depending on the market on which the shares are traded.

Comments from fund managers also indicate that liquidity can vary substantially between stock markets. Poor market liquidity can be a significant impediment to investment timing, as it may restrict the purchase or sale of shares at the appropriate time. One fund manager of a Latin American fund (Fund Manager 12) noted that in certain markets, restrictions are imposed which require investors to deposit certain sums with the central bank, deterring foreign investors from the local market, and encouraging them to trade equities on New York stock markets.

Overall, the results in this section indicate that the differences between domestic and overseas equity analysis are not as important as the distinction between analysts and fund managers. Roughly the same number of companies are followed in the UK as overseas. Interestingly, however, assuming that the sample is a representative one, geographic proximity appears to be a more influential determinant of country coverage than economic significance. Furthermore, industry specialism is becoming more prevalent than specialism by country, although regional differences still appear to be material enough to prevent completely global coverage in most cases. Finally, investors follow and trade in shares in both local stock markets and the markets where the shares have a secondary listing. The remainder of this chapter looks at how such factors may influence how domestic and overseas shares are analysed.

7.3 EQUITY ANALYSIS TECHNIQUES USED

This section examines the techniques used to analyse equities by investment analysts and fund managers. First, the techniques used by analysts and fund managers in domestic and transnational analysis are compared and contrasted. The results from analysts and fund managers who follow foreign companies are then partitioned into different groups to explore whether international variation exists.

7.3.1 Overall usefulness of analysis techniques

Table 7.8 shows that fundamental analysis is by far the most useful technique to both fund managers and analysts with an overall mean of 4.76 out of a maximum 5.00.[7] This finding is clearly in line with the findings of prior research discussed in Chapter 3. The means for analysts and fund managers

[7] The unit of analysis in Tables 7.8 to 7.11 is the number of country observations made by analysts, rather than the number of analysts themselves. In other words, where an analyst rated a particular technique as very useful in more than one country (for example, France *and* Germany) this would count as

Table 7.8 Usefulness of equity analysis techniques

	Fund managers		Investment analysts		Total	
	Mean	Std. dev.	Mean	Std. dev.	Mean	Std. dev.
Fundamental analysis	4.75	0.58	4.77	0.46	4.76	0.54
Ratio analysis	4.34	0.88	4.21	0.93	4.30	0.90
Assessment of management	4.16	0.79	4.20	0.84	4.17	0.81
DCF	3.20	1.17	2.92	1.02	3.10	1.13
EVA	3.14	1.13	2.89	1.06	3.05	1.11
Top-down†	2.99	1.28	3.14	1.02	3.05	1.19
Technical analysis	2.73	1.13	2.37	1.11	2.60	1.13
Beta analysis	2.15	1.02	2.09	0.92	2.13	0.99

† Only applies to respondents involved in foreign equity analysis.

are virtually identical and Mann-Whitney tests showed that no statistically significant differences exist between the two groups. This is consistent with Moizer and Arnold (1984) who found no significant differences in the usefulness of appraisal techniques between fund managers and analysts (both of whom regarded fundamental analysis as the most useful technique).

Overall, the top three techniques are all based on a fundamental approach to investment analysis, and the mean responses are substantially higher than the next group, i.e., discounted cash flow (DCF), economic value added (EVA) and top down. Both DCF and EVA are more useful to fund managers than to investment analysts.

The final group of techniques in Table 7.8 comprises those which rely on market data, i.e., technical analysis and beta analysis. The relative position of these techniques is consistent with prior research, as both feature as having limited utility, particularly beta analysis. Technical analysis is more useful to fund managers than to analysts, which reflects fund managers' need effectively to 'time' the investment decision accurately (e.g. Blake, 2000). The preference of fund managers for beta analysis (2.15 versus 2.09 for analysts) is also consistent with previous research and is unsurprising, given that it is based on portfolio analysis rather than individual security analysis.

two responses. The means recorded in these tables are therefore based on the number of these country observations, and not on the number of analysts.

7.4 COMPARISON OF DOMESTIC AND TRANSNATIONAL ANALYSIS TECHNIQUES

In order to assess whether international differences in accounting and financial reporting cause overseas shares to be analysed differently to domestic shares, the sample in the questionnaire survey was split into analysts who only analyse UK companies, and those who analyse overseas companies. Table 7.9 presents the results. Overall, with the exception of technical analysis and DCF analysis, there are surprisingly few differences. More specifically, fundamental analysis is by far the most influential technique in foreign company analysis, with a mean response broadly corresponding to 'extremely useful' on the 5-point scale. Furthermore, ratio analysis and managerial assessments as components of fundamental analysis are also widely used.

Prima facie, the results in Table 7.9 do not appear to indicate that analysis techniques which do not involve accounting information are more useful in transnational equity analysis than in domestic equity analysis, as found in some prior research. However, the difference between the usefulness of DCF analysis to analysts of foreign companies is apparently indicative of a greater reliance on cash flow information and dividends, rather than on earnings and book values; possibly because of lower comparability of foreign accruals-based information. This is consistent with the findings of Choi and Levich (1991). Further light is shed on this issue in the next chapter where the usefulness of different sections of overseas annual reports is examined.

Table 7.9 Usefulness of equity analysis techniques in UK and transnational analysis

	UK analysis		Transnational analysis	
	Mean	Std. dev.	Mean	Std. dev.
Fundamental analysis	4.69	0.61	4.79	0.50
Ratio analysis	4.23	0.90	4.33	0.90
Management assessment	4.15	0.81	4.18	0.81
DCF	2.96	1.00	3.16	1.17
Top-down†	n/a	n/a	3.05	1.19
EVA	3.17	1.00	3.00	1.15
Technical analysis	2.76	0.90	2.53	1.21
Beta analysis	2.13	0.94	2.13	1.01

† Only applies to respondents involved in foreign equity analysis.

The finding that technical analysis is substantially more useful in UK company analysis than in foreign company analysis is also noteworthy. Given that technical analysis does not require the use of accounting data, cross border comparisons can be made more easily with share price performance. Analysts of foreign companies were therefore expected to be more, rather than less, reliant on technical analysis relative to domestic analysts.

Although interviews confirmed the widespread use of charts for timing decisions, with the exception of analysts and fund managers involved in the Japanese and US stock markets, this use was primarily for confirmatory, rather than predictive, purposes. For example, Analyst 9 pointed out:

> Technical analysis is useful for examining the market's reaction to previous events, such as changes in management and the business cycle.

A number of reasons were suggested for the finding that technical analysis is more useful in UK equity analysis. First, many other markets do not have the necessary liquidity for technical analysis. That is, share price movements may not be frequent enough to identify trends and patterns in share prices. Second, the emphasis on sector performance rather than country performance has led to technical analysis being of limited use in some markets. Fund Manager 6, for example, noted the limitations of national stock market data:

> If you're analysing Mannesmann, what the German market does is less important than what the European market or telecoms sector does.

Three respondents stated that they do not hold technical analysis in high regard in general, (i.e., in domestic or transnational analysis) while three fund managers stated that the data necessary for technical analysis are either not available, or not reliable. For example, Fund Manager 18 noted that Japanese share price data are not always adjusted appropriately for stock splits. Fund Manager 9 had experienced inequality in the access to information necessary for technical analysis. She stated that in certain European markets, the data are not always available, and are sometimes given to certain investors before others:

> I would never base my decision on [technical analysis] but I might look at charts just to perhaps support my judgement in terms of timing buying and selling. Also I think in Europe, information is not necessarily freely available. If you take Norway for example, you don't always really know what is going on – a share will jump ahead of an announcement and that is supposed to not be able to happen. Due to insider trading and laws, everyone should have the same information at the same time, but in Europe that doesn't happen.

Fund managers and analysts involved in analysing Japanese and particularly US companies, however, expressed surprise at technical analysis being of limited use relative to domestic analysis. Analyst 10 (an institutional sales analyst who covered US companies) stated that momentum analysis is very popular in the US, while Analyst 11 (an institutional sales person analysing Japanese companies) pointed out that charts can help with selling equities if the pattern reinforces the sales advice he is making. Consistent with the findings of Olbert (1994), therefore, the use of technical analysis appears to be dependent upon the characteristics of the relevant stock exchange.

Although the top-down approach *prima facie* represents a valuable mechanism for coping with international accounting and reporting diversity, its usefulness relative to other techniques in Table 7.9 indicates that analysts of foreign companies do not consider the technique very useful. Selecting investment opportunities on the basis of market and economic factors and then focusing on company specific performance obviates the need for comparable accounting information and was therefore expected to be highly regarded. The mean of 3.05 on the scale, however, corresponds only to the 'quite useful' category in the questionnaire. This result broadly corresponds to the findings of Bhushan and Lessard (1992), who found that the top-down approach was only used by a third of fund managers. Moreover, it is consistent with the increasing focus on sector, rather than country, factors outlined earlier.

The techniques used by analysts of foreign companies therefore reflect a similar approach to analysts of UK companies; fundamental analysis is the predominant technique to both groups. The techniques which avoid non-comparable accounting data (i.e. technical analysis and the top-down approach) were expected to be very useful in transnational analysis. However, they are not remotely as popular as fundamental analysis, hence, international accounting differences do not appear to be so significant as to deter analysts or fund managers from using fundamental analysis.

7.4.1 International variation in transnational analysis techniques

As noted above, the interviews revealed a common pattern in the geographical organisation of the financial institutions. An interesting question, therefore, is the extent to which analysts of foreign companies vary their techniques depending on the country of domicile of the company being analysed. Table 7.10 presents the usefulness of the various

Table 7.10 International differences in the usefulness of analysis techniques

	Europe	Asia Pacific region	US and Canada	Emerging markets
	Mean	Mean	Mean	Mean
Fundamental analysis	4.74	4.78	4.86	4.86
Ratio analysis	4.29	4.22	4.41	4.38
Assessment of management	4.14	4.33	4.28	4.07
DCF	3.07	3.25	3.15	3.23
EVA	3.06	3.21	2.71	3.14
Top-down	3.09	3.32	2.93	3.64
Technical analysis	2.56	2.44	2.90	3.14
Beta analysis	2.03	2.38	2.45	2.13

techniques adopted in the analysis of companies in Europe, Asia (including Japan), North America and emerging markets.

The results demonstrate that the fundamental approach remains dominant across all geographic regions. Its constituents of ratio analysis and assessment of management are also highly regarded, although ratios are used marginally less for companies in the Asia-Pacific region. Analysts and fund managers who followed Japanese companies expressed reservations over the credibility of some ratios, particularly because of acute problems of asset undervaluation. Managerial assessments are used less for companies in emerging markets, which may reflect difficulties in getting access to managers as pointed out by some fund managers in the interviews. Interestingly, top-down analysis and DCF techniques are most useful in Asian and emerging markets, possibly reflecting poorer accounting disclosures.

Overall, Table 7.10 indicates that there is a high degree of similarity in the usefulness of all the techniques. The only two cases where statistically significant differences emerge between the regions in Kruskal-Wallis tests were for beta analysis and technical analysis. Although beta analysis is the least useful technique to all groups, it appears to be more useful in American company analysis. Similarly, technical analysis is most influential in the US and Canada. This result may be attributable to data availability in this region, i.e., an area characterised by particularly highly-developed stock markets, with high-frequency individual share and index data. Countries in emerging markets will typically not have such data readily available, although this is changing. Overall, however, the questionnaire data indicates that there is little international variation in the techniques used to analyse overseas companies; fundamental analysis is by far the most commonly used technique in developed and emerging markets.

The interview data, on the other hand, did point to some differences in the approach used to analyse companies between regions – sometimes within the fundamental approach. One manager of an Asian fund (Fund Manager 1) noted that the income statement is used less than the balance sheet in the analysis of some Asian companies. Also, Fund Manager 10, an emerging markets fund manager, described how DCF and top-down analysis were used largely due to a lack of availability of accounting information; this contrasted with a far more systematic fundamental approach used by him when he was in a previous job, responsible for managing a US fund.

7.5 DIFFERENCES BETWEEN TRANSNATIONAL ANALYSTS AND FUND MANAGERS

Because prior research demonstrates that differences exist between investment analysts and fund managers in a domestic context (e.g., Moizer and Arnold, 1984; Barker, 1998), the sample of analysts of overseas equities was split to see whether this finding held in a transnational context. Table 7.11 presents data on the usefulness of analysis techniques to analysts and fund managers involved in foreign company analysis.

Yet again, there appears to be a strong degree of consensus on the usefulness of fundamental analysis, which is by far the most useful technique

Table 7.11 Transnational analysis techniques used by analysts and fund managers

	Fund managers		Investment analysts		Total	
	Mean	Std. dev.	Mean	Std. dev.	Mean	Std. dev.
Fundamental analysis	4.78	0.56	4.80	0.40	4.79	0.50
Ratio analysis	4.38	0.90	4.25	0.91	4.33	0.90
Management assessment	4.17	0.80	4.20	0.81	4.18	0.81
DCF	3.38	1.24	2.81	0.96	3.16	1.17
EVA	3.08	1.22	2.87	1.02	3.00	1.15
Top-down	2.99	1.28	3.14	1.02	3.05	1.19
Technical analysis	2.71	1.23	2.25	1.13	2.53	1.21
Beta analysis	2.21	1.07	2.02	0.90	2.13	1.01

to both fund managers and analysts. However, fund managers view ratio analysis, DCF analysis and EVA as more useful than analysts. This result is consistent with a necessarily systematic approach from fund managers, compared to a more detailed and judgmental (and consequently, a more time consuming) approach from analysts.

A further result common with the aggregated results is that technical analysis is more useful to fund managers than to analysts. As conjectured earlier, this is likely to be due to the need to time accurately investment decisions. Relative to other techniques, however, technical analysis is not regarded as very useful by either analysts or fund managers. Therefore, while there are differences between analysts and fund managers in the perceived usefulness of transnational equity appraisal techniques, fundamental analysis is clearly the most useful technique to both groups when analysing foreign equities.

7.6 TRANSNATIONAL ANALYSIS TECHNIQUES: A FOCUS ON FUNDAMENTAL ANALYSIS

Given the significance attached to fundamental analysis in the questionnaire survey, analysts and fund managers were also asked to describe their decision-making process when deciding to buy, hold or sell equities of foreign firms. This was in order to gain a more detailed understanding of decision-making processes within the fundamental analysis approach.

For analysts, and as found in prior research into domestic equity analysis (e.g., Arnold and Moizer, 1984), decision making was varied, ranging from systematic to subjective and judgmental. For example, Analyst 3 (a European telecoms companies analyst) stated that he conducts a systematic analysis using discounted cash flow and multiples, such as enterprise value to earnings before interest, taxation, depreciation and amortisation (EV/EBITDA) to arrive at a valuation (where EV represents enterprise value, given by market value of equity, plus market value of debt, less the company's cash balance). This valuation is then compared with other companies in the sector. If the value is 10% above the share price, it is recommended as a 'buy' and if it is 10% lower, it is recommended as a 'sell'. However, Analyst 3 noted that this approach is used more in the telecoms sector, indicating, in line with Barker (1999) that the valuation models used may be dependent on the industry or sector of the company being analysed.

At the other end of the continuum, Analyst 6 (a European pharmaceuticals companies analyst) stated that his process is not formalised, pointing out that fundamental analysis 'is not a methodological series of instruction'.

The technique used by Analyst 6 essentially involves examining relative performance over the following six months, using valuation ratios such as P/E or EV/EBITDA against leading US and European competitors, while also allowing for country variations in multiples. Analyst 5 also pointed out that the fundamental analysis approach varied between different firms. Consistent with the findings in the previous sections of analysts moving away from country-based specialism, intra-sector comparisons of ratios and performance were prevalent in sell-side analysts' techniques, and sector-based factors clearly underpinned the basis of analysis.

Examination of fund managers' decision making revealed a multi-stage process involving other members of the institution. The first stage of the investment decision lies with a senior asset allocation committee, which allocates funds to the key regions of Europe, the US, Asia and Japan and other emerging markets, on the basis of economic variables, with reference to a global index, such as MSCI® (Morgan Stanley Capital International).

Following this allocation, most fund managers progress to a 'screening' stage in their investment process, which involves the initial selection of companies that meet certain criteria. These companies are subsequently subjected to more rigorous analysis. This screening stage would not form part of sell-side analysts' techniques, as they are devoted to a relatively small number of companies in a specific industry. Transnational fund managers, on the other hand, often have hundreds of potential investee companies in their 'universe', and thus have to find a means of discriminating between them in the initial stages in order to reduce the number of companies to a manageable figure.

The screens used by fund managers take one of two forms. The first involves discriminating on a purely quantitative basis, using a combination of factors such as company size, performance or valuation multiples such as EV/EBITDA or P/E. The second is a 'thematic' approach, where fund managers, either themselves or through analysts' research, identify themes, then ascertain how these themes will affect specific companies. In some instances, this thematic approach was necessitated by the absence of the data required for a systematic quantitative screening.

Fundamental analysis of individual companies follows this screening process. This involves an assessment of company management and strategy, a detailed analysis of financial statements and a questioning of local analysts. Thus, the approach taken by fund managers was characterised as 'bottom-up within top-down', that is, at the individual fund manager level, the analysis is company specific and bottom up, yet this analysis follows an earlier asset allocation stage. The ultimate investment decision is then made in consultation with other members of the regional 'desk' or team, who offer additional insights and knowledge.

It appears, therefore, that the use of top-down analysis has probably been understated, at least at the institutional level. This is because the questionnaire focused on the use of top-down at the individual fund manager level; here it was not perceived as useful. At the institutional level, however, top-down appears to be more prevalent, and is therefore effectively used alongside fundamental analysis, although at opposite ends of the investment decision. This also helps to explain the results of Bhushan and Lessard (1992), who found that fund managers perceive both top-down and bottom-up analysis techniques to be useful.

The interviews also included questions on the ratios used in company analysis, in order to ascertain whether differences exist between transnational analysis and domestic analysis. In domestic analysis, the P/E ratio is a dominant valuation ratio (Arnold and Moizer, 1984 and Pike *et al.*, 1993). However, international accounting differences represent a significant obstacle to the comparison of P/E ratios. Interestingly, fund managers and analysts involved in transnational analysis have devised a way of mitigating the effects of international accounting differences, by effectively 'moving up' the income statement. In particular, the EV/EBITDA ratio was referred to specifically by the majority of analysts and fund managers.

Numerous comments exemplify why this ratio is so valuable in transnational analysis. Fund Manager 12, for example, used P/E only as a tertiary indicator; he examined EV/EBITDA to strip out accounting differences, as 'there is no need to go through the accounts if you go up earnings far enough'. Similarly, Fund Manager 13 stated that:

> EV/EBITDA is used because of accounting differences in the treatment of debt, tax and depreciation, so backing up [the profit and loss account] this far gives you a better feeling of operational profitability and what is coming through in terms of that.

Fund Manager 9 commented that she uses EV/EBITDA because it is more suitable in transnational analysis, and can be used for comparing 'apples with apples'. She also pointed out that this ratio is more popular in transnational analysis due to the time involved in adjusting accounts. Similarly, Fund Manager 11 commented that country differences are not too much of a problem because:

> What you tend to do is use a ratio that gives you a better basis for cross-border comparisons, i.e., EV/EBITDA.

Overall, the number of analysts and fund managers stating they used EV/EBITDA exceeded those who stated they relied on P/E ratios by 20% (18 to 15), despite recent research indicating that P/E is, in general, the most dominant valuation ratio (Fernandez, 2001).

7.7 DISCUSSION AND CONCLUSIONS

In summary, *prima facie*, the results in this chapter indicate that diversity in international accounting and financial reporting systems does not encourage the transnational financial community to employ different overall approaches to those used in domestic analysis. In line with previous research into domestic equity analysis, transnational analysts and fund managers show a clear preference for fundamental analysis, even though this entails analysis of (typically non-comparable) accounting information and financial statements. Furthermore, ratio analysis, a key component of fundamental analysis, which may involve analysis of foreign company financial statements, is also highly regarded. With the notable exception of technical analysis being more useful in UK company analysis, there is little overall difference between the analysis techniques used by domestic and transnational analysts and fund managers. Somewhat surprisingly, the three least useful techniques to transnational analysts and fund managers are those which obviate the need for accounting data, namely top-down, technical analysis and beta analysis.

UK analysts now often analyse European companies and discussions in interviews revealed that this trend is expected to continue. This diminution of the relevance of national boundaries is reflected in a degree of uniformity in the approaches used to analyse equities. The differences between domestic and overseas analysts are not as important as those between analysts and fund managers, and possibly (as found by Barker, 1999), as those between sectors. Thus, it appears that analysts who are trained and experienced in the analysis of UK companies are applying these techniques to foreign companies.

Although there is little overall variation between domestic and transnational techniques, the interviews did reveal one difference *within* the transnational fundamental analysis technique. This is the prevalence of the use of earnings before interest, taxation, depreciation and amortisation (EBITDA), which is normally expressed in the EV/EBITDA ratio. Comments from analysts and fund managers indicate that this ratio is widely used as a means of coping with international accounting differences, many of which are avoided by this ratio.

Two points are worth noting in relation to this finding. First is the possibility that this ratio is used in company analysis in general, i.e. in domestic and transnational analysis. There is some evidence that EBITDA is becoming more widespread generally (Francis *et al.* 2003). However, comments made in the interviews signified that EV/EBITDA is particularly suited for transnational analysis and cross-border comparisons. Furthermore, recent research has shown that the Price/Earnings (P/E) ratio is far more prevalent than EV/EBITDA in domestic analysis. The prevalence of the EV/EBITDA ratio in the interviews (although across a limited sample) indicates that it is more widely used than P/E in transnational analysis.

The second point to consider is the possibility that information is lost through the exclusion of accruals and other information by 'moving up' the income statement. Recent market-based empirical research by Francis *et al.* (2003) demonstrates that a comprehensive measure of earnings (which includes accruals, interest, depreciation and taxation) is far superior to EBITDA in explaining share returns. This indicates that EBITDA-based decisions may be neglecting important information.

The results from the questionnaire survey indicated that fundamental analysis is the most useful technique in analysing overseas companies, irrespective of the geographic location of the company. However, subtle differences in the techniques used do exist and these appear to be at least partly driven by the quality of accounting data. Techniques which avoid accruals-based accounting information (DCF and top-down analysis) were perceived as relatively more useful in emerging markets and in Asian markets; beta analysis was also more useful in developed markets.

The research has highlighted differences between analysts and fund managers in the analysis of foreign firms. In particular, the interviews and questionnaires revealed that analysts specialise more by industry relative to fund managers, although increasingly, fund managers are adopting a sectoral rather than a country-based emphasis. The questionnaire results showed that fund managers find DCF techniques more useful than analysts. Fund managers' reliance on a technique, which facilitates a more systematic approach, is consistent with their responsibility for significantly greater numbers of companies than analysts, and a consequential need to reduce this to a manageable number for a more detailed analysis. Furthermore, fund managers find technical analysis more useful than analysts, which is consistent with their need effectively to time the investment decision.

The following chapter examines how international differences in financial reporting regimes manifest themselves in the different sources of information used by analysts and fund managers.

7.8 REFERENCES

Arnold, J. and Moizer, P. (1984). 'A survey of the methods used by UK investment analysts to appraise investments in ordinary shares.' *Accounting and Business Research*, **Summer**, 195–207.

Barker, R.G. (1998). 'The market for information: evidence from finance directors, analysts and fund managers.' *Accounting and Business Research*, **29** (1), 1–20.

Barker, R. (1999). 'Survey and market-based evidence of industry-dependence in analysts' preferences between the dividend yield and price-earnings ratio valuation models.' *Journal of Business Finance and Accounting*, **26** (3), 393–418.

Bhushan, R. and Lessard, D.R. (1992). 'Coping with international accounting diversity: fund managers' views on disclosure, reconciliation, and harmonization.' *Journal of International Financial Management and Accounting*, **4** (2), 149–164.

Blake, D. (2000). *Financial Market Analysis*, 2nd edn, John Wiley and Sons, Chichester.

Choi, F.D.S. and Levich, R.M. (1991). 'Behavioral effects of international accounting diversity.' *Accounting Horizons*, **June**, 1–13.

Fernandez, P. (2001). 'Valuation multiples: how do analysts reach their conclusions?' *IESE Business School Working Paper*.

Froot, K.A. and Dabora, E. (1999). 'How are stock processes affected by the location of trade?' *Journal of Financial Economics*, **53** (2), 189–216.

Francis, J., Schipper, K. and Vincent, L. (2003). 'The relative incremental explanatory power of earnings and alternative (to earnings) performance measures for returns.' *Contemporary Accounting Research*, **20** (1), 121–164.

International Monetary Fund (2000). *International Financial Statistics*, December, Washington, D.C.

London Stock Exchange (2000). *Secondary Market Fact Sheet*, December, London Stock Exchange, London.

Moizer, P. and Arnold, J. (1984). 'Share appraisal by investment analysts – portfolio vs. non-portfolio managers.' *Accounting and Business Research*, **Autumn**, 341–348.

Olbert, L. (1994). 'Stock valuation methods of financial analysts in a thin stock market in Sweden, with comparisons to the United Kingdom and the United States.' *International Journal of Accounting*, **29**, 123–135.

Pike, R., Meerjanssen, J. and Chadwick, L. (1993). 'The appraisal of ordinary shares by investment analysts in the UK and Germany.' *Accounting and Business Research*, **23** (92), 489–499.

Weetman, P., Collins, W and Davie, E. (1994). *Operating and Financial Review: Views of Analysts and Institutional Investors*, Institute of Chartered Accountants of Scotland Research Report, Edinburgh.

8
Transnational Information Sources

8.1 INTRODUCTION

The aim of this chapter is to examine how international differences in financial reporting manifest themselves in the information sources used by UK analysts and fund managers in the analysis of overseas equities. As noted in Chapter 3, international variation in accounting and financial reporting regimes is often substantial and can affect the availability and comparability of information in different countries. However, what is unclear on the basis of previous research is the extent to which this variation fosters reliance on different sources of information. For example, while Chapter 4 demonstrated that accounting information and direct company contact are the most influential sources in domestic equity analysis, there is virtually no extant research which confirms whether the same holds in transnational analysis.

The next section compares the sources used to analyse UK and overseas shares in general. This is followed by a comparison of the information used by analysts and fund managers in transnational equity analysis. The results are then split by geographic region in order to examine whether the information sources used in transnational analysis are dependent upon the origins of the company being analysed. The chapter then focuses on three specific sources found to be particularly important in overseas equity analysis, namely the annual report, direct company contact and locally-based analysts.

8.2 DOMESTIC AND TRANSNATIONAL INFORMATION SOURCES

8.2.1 Domestic equity analysis

Columns 1 and 2 of Table 8.1 present the results for the usefulness of information sources to analysts and fund managers involved in domestic company analysis; these results represent a benchmark for comparison with transnational information sources, and with prior research. In general, the results on analysts involved purely in domestic analysis are consistent with the research reviewed in Chapter 4.

Table 8.1 Usefulness of domestic and transnational information sources

	Domestic analysis		Transnational analysis		Total	
	Mean	Std. dev.	Mean	Std. dev.	Mean	Std. dev.
Company visit	4.17	0.93	4.39	0.97	4.32	0.96
Meetings with company management	4.53	0.72	4.35	0.98	4.40	0.92
Most recent company annual report	4.01	1.00	4.17	0.89	4.12	0.92
Preliminary earnings announcements	4.02	0.91	3.82	0.88	3.88	0.89
Interim company reports	3.47	0.94	3.60	1.04	3.56	1.01
Form 20-F (companies listed in the US only)	3.19	1.36	3.55	1.29	3.51	1.30
Industry statistics	3.56	0.89	3.53	0.78	3.54	0.81
Telephone calls to company	3.42	1.11	3.51	1.28	3.49	1.23
Company presentations	3.64	0.94	3.46	1.10	3.51	1.05
Previous company annual reports	3.04	1.00	3.35	1.03	3.26	1.03
Other foreign analysts' reports	n/a	n/a	3.33	1.04	3.33	1.04
Sector specialist publications	3.28	0.98	3.32	0.92	3.31	0.94
Managerial forecasts	3.22	0.95	3.28	0.96	3.26	0.96
Datastream or other equivalent sources	3.30	0.94	3.22	1.05	3.24	1.02
Macro-economic indicators	3.45	0.91	3.19	0.97	3.26	0.96
Other UK analysts' reports	3.53	0.94	3.13	1.02	3.26	1.01
Financial press	2.94	0.89	3.08	0.79	3.04	0.82
Company web-sites	2.35	0.92	2.65	0.96	2.57	0.96
Company financial PR agencies	1.93	0.70	2.04	0.81	2.01	0.78

Prima facie, three groups emerge in the rankings of the most useful domestic information sources. The first group comprises information direct from the company, including accounting information. Each of these sources has a mean response over 4.00 (i.e., management meetings, company visits, preliminary announcements and the annual report). Within this group, meetings with company management clearly represent the most useful source of information. Almost 90% of analysts and fund managers regard these meetings as either extremely useful or very useful. Although the average score for preliminary results is marginally higher than that for the annual report, the means for the two sources are virtually indistinguishable.

The next group comprises information from both the company itself (e.g., presentations and telephone calls) and from third parties (e.g., industry statistics, other analysts and *Datastream*). Industry statistics, for example, have both a median and modal value of 3.00 (not reported). The distribution of the responses for the usefulness of other analysts' reports is also noteworthy. Further investigation revealed that the relatively low mean (3.53) and high median and mode (4.00 for both) is indicative of a bimodal distribution. This is a result of grouping together fund managers and investment analysts; both have different opinions regarding the usefulness of analysts' reports – fund managers rely on such reports far more than investment analysts do.[1]

The third and final group comprises previous annual reports, financial press, company web-sites and financial public relations agencies. With the exception of previous versions of the annual report, each has a mean below the mid-point of 3, and are generally not highly regarded. PR agencies in particular are poorly placed – only 2 respondents rated them as very useful in UK company analysis.

8.2.2 Transnational equity analysis

The results on the usefulness of information sources in the analysis of foreign companies are presented in columns 3 and 4 of Table 8.1. The results indicate that geographical distance does not reduce reliance on direct company contact: company visits and management meetings are the most useful information source in transnational equity analysis. Both sources have median scores of 5, and 83% of analysts and fund managers involved in analysing foreign shares regard company visits and management meetings as very useful or extremely useful.

Table 8.1 also shows that accounting information and the annual report in particular are very well utilised in transnational equity analysis. In addition to company contact and, despite international accounting diversity, the most recent annual report and preliminary announcements clearly represent highly influential information sources in transnational investment decisions. In particular, annual reports of foreign companies, are regarded as extremely useful or very useful by over three quarters of analysts and

[1] Further analysis of the data corroborated this. The means for fund managers versus analysts were 3.75 and 3.00 respectively, and a Mann-Whitney test confirmed that the difference between analysts and fund managers is statistically significant at the 0.01 level.

fund managers. However, preliminary earnings announcements are more useful in domestic company analysis. Furthermore, previous annual reports are also significantly more useful in foreign equity analysis relative to domestic analysis, with means of 3.04 and 3.35 respectively. This may reflect a lack of other reliable information sources on foreign companies, and is consistent with the 'reference' role played by the annual report described by Holland (1998).

Table 8.1 also indicates that the usefulness of other information sources differs between domestic and transnational analysis. SEC Form 20-F is ranked as the 6th most useful source in foreign company analysis, representing an endorsement of US accounting requirements.[2] Various factors emerged from the interviews as being responsible for this result. One obvious explanation is the quality of the underlying accounting standards, i.e. the quality of accounting measurement.[3] Three analysts and three fund managers stated this as the reason. However, two additional reasons were noted. First the comparability of the information reported in Form 20-F is useful for cross-border analysis (the issue of comparability is discussed further below). Second, and most prominent, was the quality of *disclosure*. Analyst 1, for example, stated:

> The depth and quantity of information required under a US listing means that any company who has one, you look at the 20-F before you look at the home market accounts.

Analyst 2 gave a specific example of a German pharmaceutical company involved in litigation which disclosed more under Form 20-F than anywhere else. Fund Manager 2 (a Japanese fund manager) noted that Form 20-F is particularly useful for disclosures of pension underfunding which are not required under Japanese regulations. Further, Fund Manager 3 stated that the segmental disclosures are more comprehensive under US requirements than local requirements. The reasons for referring to Form 20-F therefore extend beyond the issues of rigorously-enforced measurement rules and the comparability of information.

Table 8.1 also shows that company web-sites are far more useful in foreign company analysis. This is understandable as web-sites are a low cost way for companies to attract overseas investors' who may find the acquisition of information on foreign companies more difficult than for domestic companies. Notwithstanding this, the position (ranked 18th) of such an easily

[2] Interestingly, and although based on a small number of responses (because it only pertains to respondents involved in US company analysis), SEC Form 10-K was also highly regarded, with a mean response of 3.92.

[3] Although this may have changed since the Enron/WorldCom collapses which cast a shadow over US accounting.

accessible and low cost information source as company web-sites is lower than might be expected. In the interviews, while some comments confirmed a lack of reliance on company web-sites, the prevailing view was that usage had increased substantially in the intervening period between the questionnaire survey and the interviews. This was due to improvements in the quality of information reported, advances in the technology used and increased take-up of the internet by analysts and fund managers. Interestingly, one respondent stated that he now looks first to the internet rather than to sell-side analysts, although he acknowledged that internet-based information is still limited. The growth in internet usage in transnational analysis may therefore have significant implications for sell-side analysts, in that fund managers may look increasingly to the internet instead of to sell-side analysts, particularly as the quality and levels of information disclosed by companies improve.

While reservations over the reliability of company web-sites were expressed by one emerging markets fund manager (who had spotted obvious typographical errors in some financial statements) most complaints were based on the absence of an English language translation and of any timely, relevant information. On balance, however, opinions on the current and predicted value of web-sites in transnational analysis were far more positive than implied by the questionnaire results.

A common use of web-sites is the retrieval of company annual reports and press releases. This is a valuable development for both fund managers and analysts engaged in transnational analysis as such information was far less easily obtainable before the advent of the internet. In this context, Fund Manager 11 noted:

> With European companies, [web-sites] tend to be far more important than for United Kingdom companies, because the information feeds we get here on Reuters will tell you what the profits are on some headline basis, whereas the company web-site will actually give you the whole interim report or preliminary results.

Analyst 5 also appreciated this facility, particularly as it sometimes obviated the attendance of meetings in Europe, and saved him considerable time and travel expenses.

A final point to note from Table 8.1 is that foreign based analysts' reports are ranked more highly than other UK-based analysts' reports in transnational analysis (means of 3.33 versus 3.13 respectively). Foreign analysts' research is ranked 11th, whereas UK-based analysts are ranked 16th. Therefore, when analysing foreign firms, UK-based fund managers and analysts appear to rely more on foreign analysts, possibly to overcome differences in accounting, financial reporting and disclosure practices. This is important as views on harmonisation and international accounting diversity will be shaped by the extent to which adequate information on foreign firms can be obtained by other analysts. This issue is investigated in more depth in later sections. The following section now looks at the extent to which the results on information used to analyse overseas equities are dependent on the country or region where the company is based.

8.2.3 International variation in transnational information sources

Table 8.2 presents the results on the variation in the usefulness of transnational information sources according to different regions (Europe, Asia Pacific region, the US and Canada, and emerging markets).

Both company meetings and the company annual report are significantly more useful in some regions than others (at the 0.01 and 0.05 levels respectively in Kruskal Wallis tests). In particular, both sources are perceived as less useful in Asia and in emerging markets than in the more developed markets of the US and Canada and in Europe. Furthermore, telephone contact with the company is also regarded as significantly less useful in emerging markets. Indeed, many results in Table 8.2 indicate that analysts and fund managers are more heavily reliant on information sourced from outside the company in developing markets. For instance, sector-based publications, public relations agencies and macro-economic indicators are considered significantly more useful for equities in emerging markets (at the 0.05 level or higher) than in other regions. Meanwhile, accounting information is perceived as less useful in emerging markets than elsewhere as the mean responses for the annual report (most recent and previous versions) and preliminary earnings announcements are lower here than in the other three regions. By contrast, foreign analysts' research is most highly regarded for companies in emerging markets (significant at the 0.01 level in Kruskal Wallis test).

Fund Manager 10 offered support for these findings in the interviews. He pointed out that overseas fund managers often rely on analysts for language translations and accounting translations and also to provide access to company managers. He also noted that although information sources are often less reliable than in developed markets, an investment decision still has to be made as funds have to be allocated to some companies in this region, in order to achieve the benefits of diversification outlined in Chapter 2:

> Sometimes in emerging markets, it's like: 'there are your options'. You have been given [poor] information, [poor] accounting standards and [poor] access to management, but you either invest in one of these or you don't. Sometimes, there's no choice.

Table 8.2 International differences in the usefulness of information sources

	Europe	Asia Pacific region	US and Canada	Emerging markets
	Mean	Mean	Mean	Mean
Company visit	4.29	4.37	4.48	4.36
Meetings with company management	4.48	4.06	4.36	3.93
Most recent company annual report	4.19	3.91	4.00	3.57
Preliminary earnings announcements	3.92	3.57	4.07	3.43
Interim company reports	3.55	3.62	3.51	3.64
Industry statistics	3.52	3.64	3.52	3.57
Other foreign analysts' reports	3.15	3.61	3.70	3.79
Company presentations	3.50	3.35	3.83	3.46
Telephone calls to company	3.53	3.15	3.77	2.93
Form 20-F (companies listed in the US only)	3.54	3.37	3.29	3.57
Sector specialist publications	3.25	3.33	3.57	3.86
Managerial forecasts	3.24	3.14	3.55	3.43
Previous company annual reports	3.28	3.22	3.28	2.86
Datastream or other equivalent sources	3.22	3.16	3.40	3.62
Financial press	2.99	3.19	3.25	2.86
Other UK analysts' reports	3.29	3.10	3.19	3.27
Macro-economic indicators	3.2	3.29	3.26	3.86
Company web-sites	2.55	2.31	3.00	2.54
Company financial PR agencies	1.94	2.06	2.34	2.43

One other noteworthy result from Table 8.2 is that company web-sites are most useful in the US (significant at the 0.05 level). The latter result is consistent with comments in the interviews which indicated that language barriers are responsible for limiting the potential of the internet for attracting overseas funds.

Interestingly, Table 8.2 shows that foreign analysts' reports are more useful than UK analysts' reports for European companies. However, for all other regions, it is locally-based analysts that are perceived as most useful. A Mann-Whitney test confirmed that the difference between UK analysts and foreign analysts for European companies is significant at the 0.01 level. This result is likely to be due to the increased European focus of UK-based analysts discussed in Chapter 7; i.e., UK analysts are now less frequently involved solely in the analysis of UK companies – they are increasingly required to follow companies from European countries on a sectoral basis. Indeed, it is an apparent endorsement of the institutional changes, as it suggests that the analysis from a UK base is superior to that conducted in the local market.

8.3 DIFFERENCES BETWEEN TRANSNATIONAL ANALYSTS AND FUND MANAGERS

Because of the findings of previous research reviewed in Chapter 2, which demonstrates the differences between fund managers and analysts in domestic analysis (Moizer and Arnold, 1984; Barker, 1998), this section compares the information sources used by fund managers and investment analysts in overseas company analysis. Table 8.3 presents the results.

Investment analysts' most influential sources take the form of direct company communication, either personal (such as meetings and company visits) or documentary (such as the annual report and preliminary results). The annual report (both the most recent and previous versions), preliminary announcements, company presentations and telephone calls to the company are all significantly more useful to investment analysts than to fund managers. Furthermore, the annual report is the highest ranked information source to analysts of overseas companies.

The finding that presentations are more useful to analysts than to fund managers is consistent with prior research into domestic analysis (Barker, 1998), as is the importance of company visits and management meetings. While fund managers also use information direct from the company, (e.g., management meetings, company visits and the annual report) they additionally rely on third party research in the form of foreign analysts' reports, which are their 4th most useful source. This disparity in the ratings of foreign analysts between fund managers and analysts is perhaps slightly surprising in the context of transnational analysis, as one might also expect UK-based analysts to rely on foreign (locally) based analysts for relevant information on foreign firms. The role of foreign analysts in transnational analysis is examined in more detail below.

A further interesting result from Table 8.3 is the difference between transnational investment analysts and fund managers in respect of the usefulness of meetings with management. Fund managers rate such meetings

Table 8.3 Transnational information sources used by analysts and fund managers

	Fund managers		Investment analysts		Total	
	Mean	Std. dev.	Mean	Std. dev.	Mean	Std. dev.
Meetings with company management	4.41	1.02	4.26	0.92	4.35	0.98
Company visit	4.31	1.07	4.51	0.77	4.39	0.97
Most recent company annual report	3.92	0.96	4.57	0.60	4.17	0.89
Other foreign analysts' reports	3.74	0.84	2.67	1.00	3.33	1.04
Preliminary earnings announcements	3.64	0.80	4.08	0.93	3.82	0.88
Industry statistics	3.54	0.63	3.50	0.97	3.53	0.78
Form 20-F (companies listed in the US only)	3.51	1.27	3.59	1.30	3.55	1.29
Interim company reports	3.50	0.89	3.75	1.23	3.60	1.04
Other UK analysts' reports	3.44	0.93	2.71	0.98	3.13	1.02
Datastream or other equivalent sources	3.34	0.98	3.05	1.13	3.22	1.05
Company presentations	3.33	1.11	3.70	1.03	3.46	1.10
Managerial forecasts	3.32	0.95	3.20	0.98	3.28	0.96
Telephone calls to company	3.31	1.23	3.81	1.29	3.51	1.28
Macro-economic indicators	3.27	0.98	3.06	0.93	3.19	0.97
Sector specialist publications	3.24	0.89	3.43	0.96	3.32	0.92
Financial press	3.12	0.72	3.02	0.89	3.08	0.79
Previous company annual reports	3.00	0.97	3.88	0.88	3.35	1.03
Company web-sites	2.65	0.99	2.65	0.92	2.65	0.96
Company financial PR agencies	2.08	0.85	1.98	0.73	2.04	0.81

as their most useful source, whereas analysts consider them the third most useful, after the annual report and company visits. Analyst 9 confirmed in the interviews that fund managers prefer meetings with management; he noted that 'such meetings are very fashionable on the buy-side – more so than before'.

8.4 THE ROLE OF ACCOUNTING INFORMATION IN TRANSNATIONAL ANALYSIS

The research reviewed in Chapter 4 indicates quite clearly that accounting information, in particular the annual report, is relied upon very heavily in domestic equity analysis. The results in Tables 8.1, 8.2 and 8.3 appear to confirm that such information is considered useful in overseas equity analysis. This section explores this issue by examining the use of accounting information in more depth.

8.4.1 Number of annual reports analysed

Some descriptive statistics on the number of annual reports analysed by analysts and fund managers involved in both domestic and foreign company analysis are presented in Table 8.4. The mean values are pulled upwards by outliers, as the distribution is skewed by a small number of high values. Unlike the number of companies followed, differences in the average and median number of annual reports studied are driven less by fund manager versus analyst differences. For example, there is no significant difference between the average number of UK reports studied by fund managers and analysts (79 versus 62; $p = 0.237$ in a two tailed t-test). For foreign annual reports, however, fund managers study significantly more annual reports than analysts (64 versus 27 respectively; $p = 0.004$).

8.4.2 Versions of the annual report used in foreign company analysis

Depending on the size, listing status and domicile of the company being analysed, analysts and fund managers have at their disposal various versions of the annual report and financial statements. In particular, many large companies translate their annual reports into English (where applicable), and

Table 8.4 Number of annual reports studied per year†

	Fund managers		Investment analysts		Total	
	UK reports	Foreign reports	UK reports	Foreign reports	UK reports	Foreign reports
Mean	79	64	62	27	72	50
Median	50	45	35	20	50	30
Standard Deviation	71.0	68.6	107.26	34	86.9	60.1

† Based on the responses from 260 fund managers and 120 investment analysts.

Table 8.5 Use of annual reports in local and English language†

	Never		Sometimes		Always		Total
	No.	%	No.	%	No.	%	No.
Foreign language version of annual report	182	58.3	94	30.1	36	11.5	312
English language version of annual report	10	2.4	88	21.4	313	76.2	411

† Based on the responses from the 155 analysts involved in transnational analysis.

sometimes prepare translations of financial statements into 'more familiar' accounting standards and currencies. Tables 8.5 and 8.6 show investment analysts' and fund managers' preferences of linguistic and presentational formats of the annual report and financial statements.

8.4.2.1 Language of annual reports

Table 8.5 shows that there is an overwhelming preference for the English language version of the annual report and, similarly, limited use of the foreign language versions. The foreign language version is always used by only 11.5%, yet the English language version (where available) is always used by 76%.

Analysts and fund managers therefore appear to be heavily reliant upon the translation of annual reports. An interesting question is to what extent the absence of an English version of the annual report results in UK-based analysts and fund managers avoiding companies. The results in Table 8.5 suggest that the absence of an English translation in non-English speaking countries may well deter analysts and fund managers from investigating certain overseas companies further.

8.4.2.2 Use of local and translated financial statements

Table 8.6 shows that financial statements prepared under local accounting standards are the most widely used in transnational analysis. There is also relatively little use of financial statements translated to UK GAAP. This is likely to be a reflection of the lack of availability of such translations, as the London Stock Exchange does not require companies to translate or reconcile their accounts to UK GAAP.[4] Consistent with the prominence of SEC Form 20-F in Table 8.1, US GAAP translations are more widespread, which may

[4] Provided companies meet minimum disclosure requirements and comply with certain accounting conventions (e.g., consolidated accounts).

Table 8.6 Accounting standards used[†]

	Never		Sometimes		Always		Total
	No.	%	No.	%	No.	%	No.
Financial statements using domestic GAAP	16	4.3	165	44.8	187	50.8	368
Financial statements translated to UK GAAP	160	54.6	113	38.6	20	6.8	293
Financial statements translated to US GAAP	58	16.6	243	69.4	49	14.0	385
Financial statements translated to International Accounting Standards	77	22.5	220	64.3	45	13.2	342

[†] Based on the responses from the 155 analysts involved in transnational analysis.

be related to such financial statements being more widely available, due to the stringent SEC reconciliation and disclosure requirements.

Interestingly, local accounting standards are most popular; over 50% of analysts and fund managers in Table 8.6 always use financial statements prepared under domestic (local) accounting standards, yet only 14% and 13.2% always use those under US GAAP and IAS respectively. This is also likely to reflect the relative availability of the different versions of financial statements, i.e., local statements will always be available (provided the annual report is available), whereas IAS or US GAAP-based statements will not. This is particularly the case where the relevant overseas companies are not listed on a major stock market that requires reconciliations to US or IAS accounting principles.

It is also noteworthy that little difference exists between the prevalence of US GAAP and IAS – both are used by a large proportion of analysts and fund managers. Almost 85% use financial statements translated to US GAAP at least sometimes; the corresponding figure for IAS is 78%. The popularity of recognisable accounting standards may result from demand for comparable information between companies from different countries, or a lack of familiarity with local accounting standards.

8.4.2.3 How the annual report is used in transnational equity analysis

The decision-making processes of analysts and fund managers involved in foreign company analysis revealed that accounting information in general, and the annual report in particular, play an important role in various stages of the investment decision. As noted in Chapter 7, fund managers' initial screening stage often involves accounting variables – either absolute levels or financial ratios and multiples. Moreover, the comprehensive fundamental analysis undertaken by analysts and fund managers also involves rigorous analysis of financial statements and ratios. Discussions with analysts and fund mangers revealed that the annual report is a primary information source in its own right, but it also fulfils various other roles, particularly as an introduction to a company and as a source of questioning management in meetings. Significantly, the annual report plays an essential part in transnational investment decisions as a confirmatory device.

For fund managers, the annual report is a useful means of making initial enquiries about specific firms, particularly if limited analysts' research information is available. Fund Manager 6 stated that while the annual report is one of many information sources

> it is your legally accurate and audited source of information – it's the bottom line. If you want to go back to the basic level, the annual report has to always be there.

The various types of information published in the annual report make it a useful research tool in its own right, and for further, more comprehensive analysis. Fund Manager 7 stated that 'the annual report is useful for making sure what we are putting down in our books is genuine, or as near as we can get to it'. As is the case in domestic decisions, however, the annual report is not the only source used, and fund managers stated it is used as a means of devising questions for other sell-side analysts or company management. Fund Manager 12 noted 'if one were to go to a meeting with only one piece of data it would invariably be the annual report'. The annual report is also used to acquire information on continuing company performance, after the investment has been made. For example, Fund Manager 18 stated that the annual report is required as soon as it is available for companies that are owned, to update spreadsheets, and to check the company is continuing to perform well.

Investment analysts also use the annual report as a device for further questioning. However, due to the closer relationship between analysts and the companies they cover, the annual report is used more as a basis for forecasting financial information for companies with which they are already familiar. Comments from analysts reinforced the questionnaire result that the annual report is an essential information source. Analyst 2, for example, stated:

> The annual report is very important. It is the most information in any one place, whether you get it from the internet, whether you have it in written form, or whether they send it to you on a disk. I would not go and see a company if I had not read the annual report. If I get an idea, the first place I go is to the annual report. It is essential.

Although it was viewed as a useful benchmark document, the annual report also attracted a degree of criticism, relating primarily to the lack of timeliness and the lack of forward-looking information, both of which have been identified in domestic based research. Overall, however, it was clear from the interviews that the annual report is of critical importance in transnational analysis. It represents a useful information source in itself; and for fund managers, it supplements and helps verify information acquired from the two other main information sources, company management and investment analysts.

8.4.3 The usefulness of components of annual reports

While Tables 8.1 to 8.3 show that the annual report is a useful document in the analysis of overseas companies, what they do not reveal is the extent to which analysts and fund managers rely on the financial statements and/or on other information that may be less affected by international accounting differences. The questionnaire and interviews therefore included questions on the usefulness of components of the annual report. Table 8.7 shows the results of splitting respondents into those involved in analysing domestic companies and those who analyse foreign companies.

There is no evidence that the financial statements' utility is reduced for overseas analysts. However, narrative information is more important in analysing foreign companies than UK companies, as the operating and financial review is significantly more useful in transnational analysis.

The results show that the three financial statements and segmental information are clearly the most important components of the annual report to both groups. However, the relative ranking of these different sources shows that different types of information are used to analyse foreign versus domestic companies. The income statement is still considered very useful (mean response of 4.39) and relatively more useful (at $p < 0.01$) for foreign companies than for UK companies. Moreover, the cash flow statement is also perceived as very useful in both domestic and transnational analysis. Interestingly, Table 8.7 shows that the most important part of the annual report in transnational analysis is the consolidated balance sheet, whereas domestic company analysts and fund managers rate the cash flow statement as most useful. This is in contrast to the most recent UK research into domestic equity analysis which shows the balance sheet to be the least useful of the financial statements (e.g., Barker, 2001). Mann-Whitney tests revealed that the balance sheet is considered significantly more useful in foreign company analysis than in domestic company analysis at the 0.01 level, implying a focus on company value and stability, rather than on company

Table 8.7 Usefulness of components of annual reports

	Domestic analysis		Transnational analysis	
	Mean	Std. dev.	Mean	Std. dev.
Group balance sheet	4.20	0.77	4.50	0.66
Cash flow statement or equivalent	4.44	0.77	4.47	0.72
Group income statement/equivalent	4.04	0.88	4.39	0.75
Segmental information	4.20	0.68	4.24	0.76
Notes regarding accounting policies	3.85	0.93	4.02	0.95
Operating and financial review or equivalent	3.81	0.84	4.02	0.79
Review of operations	3.69	0.86	3.75	0.88
Financial review	3.65	0.87	3.73	0.87
Report of management board or equivalent	3.36	1.03	3.56	0.94
Chairman's/president's statement/equivalent	3.40	1.00	3.48	1.01
Summary statistics or figures	3.10	0.95	3.48	0.97
Statement of total recognised gains and losses	3.03	0.97	3.44	1.15
Historical summary	3.16	0.91	3.36	0.95
Principal subsidiary and associated undertakings	2.90	0.92	3.21	1.02
Shareholder information	2.89	0.96	3.16	1.09
Graphs and charts	2.81	0.90	3.04	1.05
Corporate governance information	2.38	1.04	2.44	1.14
Auditors' report	2.32	0.98	2.30	1.12

growth, which is typically captured by information reported in the income statement and/or the cash flow statement.

The interviewees attributed the primary ranking of the balance sheet to various factors. First, and common to both domestic and transnational analysis, the balance sheet is important in performance measurement for determining the levels of capital invested in ratios such as return on capital employed (ROCE) and return on equity (ROE). Second, the balance sheet acts as an indicator of corporate financing. Thus, information on capital structure, minority interests, changes in shareholders' funds and reserves is contained in the balance sheet. While these details are also important in domestic company analyses, respondents commented that in transnational analysis, information on corporate financing patterns is particularly useful in assessing the protection of equity investments, particularly in countries where equity is not the primary source of finance. For example, Fund Manager 9 stated that levels of external ownership (i.e. minority interests) relative to internal funds can act as a barometer for the company's attitude to outside investors:

> [The balance sheet] gives you a picture of the nature of the company, of the culture of the company – whether it is very conservative, whether it is run for the benefits of shareholders, or whether there is a family ownership structure where they don't care what earnings are.

The third function of the balance sheet in transnational analysis is as a means to deriving cash flow. In UK company analysis, such information is provided explicitly in the cash flow statement, as required by FRS1. It was clear from respondents that the reporting of such information by overseas companies was not always sufficient or presented satisfactorily. For example, Analyst 9 (a European steel companies analyst) commented:

> The balance sheet is useful for foreign companies as they do not always give you the cash flow information in the way you would like, so you can derive cash flow from the balance sheet.

Fund Manager 1 also noted that 'cash flow statements (if there is one) are often unreliable or in an unusual format, especially in Asia and Europe'. Similarly, Fund Manager 18 stated that he is not always able to obtain cash flow data, so the balance sheet may be used.

The fourth reason for the importance of transnational balance sheet relates to the perception of fund managers and analysts of the deficiencies of the income statement. Two analysts and six fund managers commented that the income statement is less reliable than the balance sheet, and in some cases, this related to specific countries or regions. Analyst 1 stated:

> There is a view in some markets in particular, because of high tax rates and large tax allowances and different treatments of goodwill and amortisation, that the P&L is more prone to manipulation and the balance sheet is therefore more important.

The final function of the balance sheet has implications beyond the immediate issue of the use of a particular component of the annual report as it appeared to be symptomatic of a defensive attitude peculiar to transnational investment, here, the integrity of investment in terms of security is apparently of greater importance than company growth, as measured by the income statement. This is in line with the extra dimension of risk in transnational investment, comprising differences in financial accounting, reporting, legal and business environments.

The use of the balance sheet was dominated by concerns about viability and liquidity as opposed to performance measures. Thus, fund managers raised concerns over company debt and tangible assets, especially cash. Analysis of debt levels are likely to be of particular importance in transnational analysis due to the additional foreign exchange risk. Investors are therefore particularly concerned with the underpinnings of the investment, sometimes at the expense of profitability. Fund Manager 3, for example, stated that in certain countries, companies with a healthy cash balance trade at a significant premium due to the perception of risk by local and foreign investors. However, rather than focus entirely on company value, the defensive approach is characterised by the establishment of higher hurdles in terms of security of the investment, as exemplified by the following quote:

> Firstly, you take a look at survivability in the balance sheet, and then you take a view of earnings, prospects and cash flow prospects. It's not that the profit and loss account is less valuable, the balance sheet is more. (Fund manager 1).

Inter alia, therefore, the balance sheet is seen as a 'safety net' in transnational investment. The following quotes sum up its role and significance:

> The balance sheet is the best guide to financial strength and should be the basis on which any investment is made. You can tell from the balance sheet almost immediately if there is something wrong. (Analyst 2)

> The balance sheet is a defence check that the firm is not going bust or if it is a highly grown company, that it can finance its growth. It is one of the first things we look at as a check that the foundations are good. (Fund Manager 9).

Two further results from Table 8.7 worthy of specific attention are the relative usefulness of the notes to the accounts, and shareholder information. That details of accounting policies in the notes to the accounts are more useful in analysing foreign companies is unsurprising, given that, on average, fund managers and analysts analyse companies from a number of different countries. Therefore, reference to the bases on which the financial statements are prepared will be more important, as there will be more variation in accounting treatments than in purely domestic analysis. Information on foreign company shareholders is the 15th most useful source in transnational analysis and is more useful (at the 0.05 level) in analysing foreign companies than UK companies. This information is relevant for ascertaining the levels of a) institutional ownership, and b) foreign investor ownership. Both of these may be useful guides to the priorities given to institutional investors and analysts in terms of disclosure and access to management. In countries which, in general, do not give equity shareholders and institutional investors priority and/or access to financial information, details of prior institutional investment may be useful for gauging individual companies' attitudes towards shareholders.

8.4.4 Usefulness of components of transnational annual reports: differences between analysts and fund managers

Table 8.8 presents the results for investment analysts and fund managers on the usefulness of transnational annual reports. Of the 23 components listed, 16 main differences exist. The key financial statements for foreign companies are significantly more useful to investment analysts than to fund managers, as is the statement of total recognised gains and losses. In addition,

Table 8.8 Usefulness of components of transnational annual reports

	Fund managers		Investment analysts	
	Mean	Std. dev.	Mean	Std. dev.
Group balance sheet	4.38	0.73	4.68	0.49
Cash flow statement or equivalent	4.49	0.65	4.45	0.82
Group income statement/equivalent	4.27	0.77	4.57	0.69
Segmental information	4.16	0.78	4.37	0.70
Notes regarding accounting policies	3.97	0.94	4.10	0.96
Operating and financial review or equivalent	3.85	0.81	4.28	0.67
Review of operations	3.68	0.97	3.85	0.71
Financial review	3.56	0.93	3.98	0.70
Report of management board or equivalent	3.57	0.93	3.54	0.95
Chairman's/president's statement/equivalent	3.51	1.03	3.43	0.99
Summary statistics or figures	3.55	0.96	3.36	0.98
Statement of total recognised gains and losses	3.20	1.07	3.80	1.17
Historical summary	3.32	0.95	3.42	0.95
Principal subsidiary and associated undertakings	3.06	1.01	3.46	1.00
Shareholder information	3.14	1.12	3.19	1.04
Graphs and charts	2.91	1.09	3.24	0.97
Corporate governance information	2.65	1.10	2.13	1.13
Auditors' report	2.40	1.12	2.13	1.10

more detailed segmental and financial information provided in segmental breakdowns, details of subsidiaries and associated companies and the operating and financial review are also more useful to investment analysts.

The consolidated balance sheet is rated as the most useful source to investment analysts (mean of 4.68), followed by the consolidated income statement (mean of 4.57), then the cash flow statement. There is no evidence, therefore, that analysts subordinate accruals-based accounting information to cash flow information in order to mitigate the effects of international accounting differences. In contrast, fund managers prefer to rely on the cash flow statement when analysing foreign firms. However, the mean responses for the three financial statements and the notes to accounts indicate that these are all very useful to both analysts and fund managers.

Overall, though, important differences exist between analysts and fund managers involved in foreign company analysis in respect of most sections of the annual report. Analysts find the balance sheet and income statement the most useful sources (with mean responses corresponding to 'extremely useful'), whereas fund managers prefer cash flow based information. However, whereas overall, analysts consider notes on accounting policies more useful than fund managers, in transnational analysis, no such difference exists. This suggests that both analysts and fund managers consider details of the bases on which overseas financial statements are prepared to be valuable for their decision making.

8.5 COMPANY CONTACTS: USES AND LIMITATIONS

Along with accounting information, and in line with prior research into domestic analysis (e.g., Barker, 1998; Holland, 1998), the questionnaire results showed that company visits and meetings with management are essential information sources to both analysts and fund managers when analysing foreign companies. Respondents were therefore asked to elaborate on what such meetings and visits entail, the frequency of meetings with management, and any difficulties they had in gaining access to foreign company management. Virtually all fund managers consider meetings with all companies in their portfolios to be essential at least once a year. Sell-side analysts typically met management more frequently. The average number of visits per company was around two per annum, although there is some variation, especially for analysts, who make more *ad hoc* visits.

Meetings with management take place both in the companies' country of domicile, and in the UK.[5] Specifically, analysts and institutional sales

[5] Two sell-side analysts also attended some meetings in New York, even though they only analyse European companies.

departments organise visits of company management to the UK. Sell-side analysts mostly attend meetings in the local country, because, as pointed out by Analyst 1, companies almost always have a meeting at home, but not always in London. Sell-side analysts also attend company presentations on company results announcements. One analyst (Analyst 6) noted that he preferred presentations to one-to-one meetings because the responses to questions are on the public record and he prefers to see how managers respond to questions in public.

A stated key objective of company visits and managerial meetings is to form an opinion of senior managements' capabilities. This is consistent with the results in Chapter 7, which showed that subjective assessments of management are very useful in foreign company analysis. A further important objective is to develop personal relationships, which were considered important to both fund managers and to analysts. A quote from Analyst 2 is illustrative:

> Many is the time I bought a company because I trusted the management to turn it around. Many is the company that I have rejected because I know more about the company than he does. There are too many people who think that this is a mechanical business, and it's not. It is a people business.

Fund managers' visits to companies are generally conducted during 'block visits' to the country or region involved. Such visits typically last from two to six weeks, and involve intensive schedules of management meetings, company visits and presentations, organised by local analysts or their employers. Such itineraries are organised in an effort to maximise productivity in the local country or region, due to the significance of travel costs.[6] Fund managers expressed a clear preference for one-to-one meetings with management, and tried to avoid having analysts present. This is because company managers are perceived as less reticent when analysts are absent from meetings, due to the release of analysts' research into the public domain.

Although foreign company managers are increasingly travelling to the UK in order to meet with institutional investors, as shown in Table 8.3, both analysts and fund managers feel that it is still important to visit the company. This is despite concerns over the time and expense involved. The primary reason is that company visits 'bring the company to life', and help in the general understanding of the company (e.g., company management, operations and personnel).

[6] Travel costs do not appear to be trivial in transnational analysis, as three respondents mentioned such expenses as an important consideration.

> Visits are quite useful to see what sort of person they employ, the type of managers, how clean the place is – the way it works. They are useful to see the technology in action, which is helpful. Company visits are a very important part of the analyst's job. (Analyst 2).

In addition to providing a general understanding, company visits provide an opportunity to obtain information which may not be attainable from meetings in the UK, for a number of reasons. For example, Fund Manager 6 (manager of a European fund) pointed out:

> We still go on company visits because you have to go and see what is happening in the factories, and meet the people. Company management are much more relaxed on their own territory. Company visits are very important. You don't necessarily make trading decisions when you come back from them, but they are an integral part of the overall process. Companies are prepared and drilled at results time. They may say the same story over and over again, so it's good to see them out of that road show environment.

Company visits are also important in order to corroborate financial analyses. For example, Fund Manager 19 spoke of the need to 'kick the tyres' on a company visit. Finally, company visits are useful for contact with personnel other than senior management. Lower management and operational staff are perceived as less reticent than senior managers, and are often unprepared (or not 'briefed') by the investor relations department.

Overall, therefore, meeting company management and other company personnel, both in the local region, or in the UK, represents a crucial source of information to both analysts and fund managers. As found in research into domestic equity analysis (e.g., Barker, 1998; Holland, 1998), they play an important role in many stages of the investment process – at the initial investment stage, where visits are made in order to acquire an initial impression of the company's management, staff and operations, and at the post-investment stage, where regular contact is maintained.

8.6 THE ROLE OF LOCAL ANALYSTS

It became immediately apparent in the interviews that while accounting information and direct management contact are very important, they are not used in isolation; rather they are complementary and are supplemented by the services and research provided by locally-based analysts. This is particularly so for companies outside Europe.

A consistent pattern emerged of how fund managers and sell-side analysts operate and inter-relate in transnational investment analysis. This was developed after discussions with participants in the earlier interviews, and

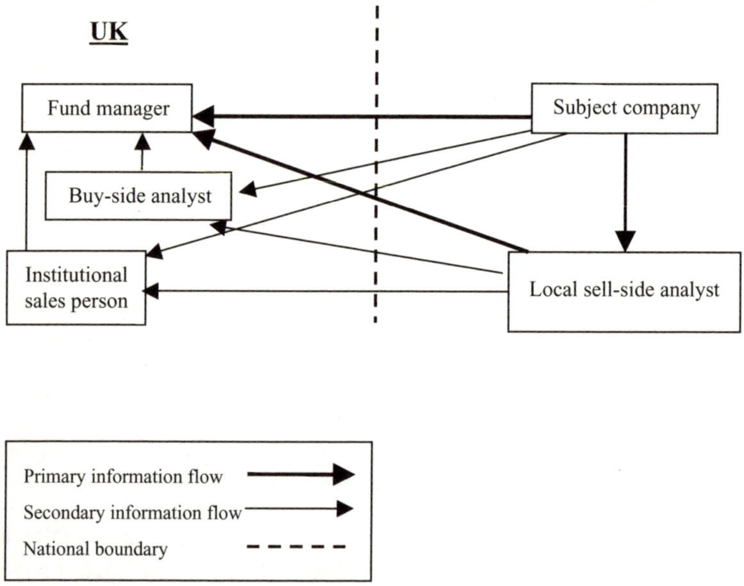

Figure 8.1 Information flows in transnational equity analysis

confirmed and verified in consultation with analysts and fund managers in the remainder of the interviews. The variety in the roles performed by the respondents (i.e., sell-side analysts, analysts involved with institutional sales, buy-side analysts and fund managers) proved very useful in acquiring different perspectives on the inter-relationships between analysts and fund managers. Figure 8.1 presents a diagram that describes how the information typically flows between the various parties involved.

In Figure 8.1, companies are the initial source of information, while fund managers are the ultimate recipients of the information. As can be seen in the diagram, however, while the information flowing directly from companies to fund managers is a primary information flow (i.e., one of the most influential and well-used), it represents only one of many information flows. First, sell-side analysts acquire, analyse and disseminate information, which may then be received either by fund managers, by in-house (buy-side) analysts in the fund managers' organisation, or by institutional sales persons (typically employed in the analysts' organisation).[7] In turn,

[7] One institutional sales person (Analyst 10) noted that while he was not supposed to use other houses' research, he did sometimes refer to it.

buy-side analysts and institutional sales persons conduct further analysis and then supply this information to fund managers.

However, in line with the changing structures of the financial institutions discussed in Chapter 7, these relationships are dynamic; the roles of the various participants are evolutionary, rather than static. In particular, the institutional sales persons interviewed felt that there is increasing pressure on them to 'add value' to the information produced by analysts. Furthermore, fund managers felt that institutional sales persons will have a diminishing role as fund managers are increasingly using information technology to communicate directly with locally-based analysts. The extent to which this substitution takes place is, however, clearly dependent on the constraints on analysts' time.

As shown in Figure 8.1, locally-based investment analysts play a crucial role in transnational analysis. This is an important finding as local expertise and company access can mitigate many of the information asymmetries between local investors and foreign investors. In particular, cultural, linguistic and accounting barriers can be reduced or avoided by regular correspondence with local sell-side analysts. Fund Manager 6 articulated why locally-based analysts are so useful for foreign company analysis:

> They understand local accounting better, they follow the companies for longer, they have more experience of the companies, they have more frequent access to management (because often management will do presentations in the local country rather than coming to London). And they have better access to management. It's the language. And if the chief executive says 'we are going to do well next year' [local analysts] know if he means he's going to do well.

Therefore, while in certain respects, the role of sell-side analysts in transnational investment analysis is comparable to their domestic role, in various other respects, they fulfil other supplementary functions. Numerous fund managers cited the acquisition and dissemination of specialist company and sector knowledge as a reason for using analysts. This function is common to both domestic and transnational analysis. The above quote, however, suggests that locally-based analysts provide functions incremental to this.

Local analysts were also viewed as being knowledgeable about, and responsive to, developments in foreign markets, relative to analysts based in the UK.

> Take Switzerland for example, the local market will know that something is going on that you might not know in London. All the information is public, but they get a better feel for what is going on locally. (Fund Manager 9)

Fund Manager 11 also noted:

> I think with European companies, it is an advantage to have someone who is actually there, because in some industries, there's a lot of consolidation going on. So an analyst who is actually there meeting the companies gets an edge.

In addition, costs of collecting detailed company-specific transnational information are reduced significantly by the obviation of frequent meetings and visits to foreign companies.

> If you need to ask a company questions, you e-mail [the analyst] and they get the answer. You need somebody to go and ask management face-to-face, so you are in control. (Fund Manager 12)

Importantly, the vast majority of fund managers rely heavily on local analysts for interpretation and analysis of accounting information. Of the 20 fund managers interviewed, 14 (70%) stated that they rely on local analysts for the interpretation of foreign accounting information. Moreover, of the remaining 6 fund managers, all rely on local analysts for general company research, which is also likely to contain analysis and interpretation of accounting information. Therefore, 70% is likely to be a conservative estimate. This helps to explain why foreign accounting information is rated so highly in the questionnaire survey, despite being based on unfamiliar accounting principles. Fund managers analyse financial statements themselves, and they also do so with the assistance of local analysts' interpretation and scrutiny of the same information.

Another function of locally-based analysts is the provision of access to companies and to top level management. Local analysts have strong links with company management, which is very useful to fund managers based in a different country. Analysts and their employers (large investment houses and stockbrokers) also facilitate fund managers' visits to foreign countries by arranging meetings and providing itineraries for the visits. These meetings may be either for foreign company management visiting the UK, or for UK fund managers visiting companies abroad. This is clearly an important role because (as the questionnaire results show) fund managers regard company contact as a vital information source. It is also important because variation in the priority given to shareholders between countries may mean that company contact is difficult to obtain.[8]

[8] For example, the prior literature in Chapter 3 and comments received in the current research show that attitudes to equity investors differ significantly between regions.

8.6.1 Information asymmetries as a cause of reliance on local analysts

Consistent with Gehrig (1993), information asymmetries appear to be significant impediments to overseas investment; these difficulties are partly responsible for the heavy reliance on local analysts. Even the most important information sources were sometimes inaccessible from a UK base. Fund manager 1, for example, noted that annual reports for Asian companies were not always readily available from London. Fund managers involved in the analysis of emerging markets also faced additional difficulties in that there was a *general* lack of information. That is, in addition to the disadvantages faced by foreign investors, the local information set is far from comprehensive. Fund Manager 10 stated:

> A lot of companies don't produce [the annual report] in English. If I have it I will definitely use it and I will try and get hold of one if I can, but sometimes I just can't. When I was a US fund manager I would not buy a company without at least reading the last annual report – it was considered a necessity. Now you are not going to get one in Egypt no matter how hard you try. It's one of the risks of emerging markets.

Access to foreign company management is also a matter of concern for fund managers. Although other factors were mentioned,[9] the ability to meet senior company management is dependent to a large extent on the country or region involved, due to variation in attitudes to shareholders. Except for extremely large US firms, fund managers involved in the analysis of US companies find gaining access to management unproblematic. For example, Fund Manager 4 (a US small company fund manager) stated that he does not have any difficulties in gaining access to US company management because US managers are heavily incentivised by options, and therefore 'they know what spins the wheel'. Fund managers and analysts involved in the analysis of companies from Asia and Europe, however, do not find managerial access so easy to obtain. Analyst 3, (a European telecoms analyst) stated:

> In general, I would say that European companies are less easy in terms of access to management because they are not used to talking to equity analysts, because they are not 'grown' into an equity culture.

[9] Other factors mentioned were subject company size (larger companies, more cooperative); institution size (larger institutions, easier access); and macro-economic conditions (poor economic conditions, easier access).

However, this lack of investor relations sophistication in Europe was regarded as a virtue by Analyst 9 who stated that:

> Foreign companies are less compulsive in telling you what to think than Anglo-Saxon companies, who try and tell you 'our profits are going to be 100 million' and that's it. So they try and get the analyst to think in one way, or not at all (and usually succeed). European companies don't want to do that so much. They are either more honest or less sophisticated, whichever way you want to put it.

In general, though, there was less sympathy for lack of investor relations. In particular, all fund mangers and analysts involved in Japanese company analysis stated that it is very difficult to gain access to Japanese company management, and that Japanese investor relations are particularly poor.

However, despite all the benefits that it brings, fund managers regard sell-side analysts' relationship with company management as a 'double edged sword'. Virtually all fund managers viewed analysts' recommendations on shares as positively biased (manifested by a dearth of sell recommendations) because analysts are reluctant to jeopardise their relationship with management for fear of losing access to the company. Fund Manager 17, for example, gave examples of US companies taking punitive action on analysts who had issued sell recommendations by restricting access:

> If you are an analyst and you write something deprecating about [Company X], your company is cut off. You won't be invited to analyst meetings by the management. Because you can't say anything bad about [Company X] – that is the power that these big blue chip firms have.

Analyst 5 (a sell-side analyst of European leisure and hotel companies) also acknowledged that issuing sell recommendations results in difficulties in gaining access to management.

Fund managers expressed further concerns over analyst independence. Analysts were perceived as reluctant to issue 'sell' recommendations due to the fear of their employers losing lucrative advisory or underwriting work. This perceived lack of independence was also acknowledged by analysts themselves:

> Too many analysts and the companies they represent make their decision on the amount of corporate work that they are doing for that company. It is a fact

> of life that you cannot ignore. Too often (and this is so prevalent in American houses) you see a 'Buy' recommendation come out on a stock, just before a major piece of corporate action is about to take place. (Analyst 2)

This presents an interesting dilemma for fund managers involved in transnational analysis. While locally-based analysts are one of fund managers' primary sources of information on foreign firms, and a key facilitator of foreign management access, the perceived lack of analysts' objectivity militates against their reliability. Thus, there is effectively a cost attached to the information provided to fund managers by analysts; certain information communicated to fund managers (in particular recommendations on shares) is potentially biased, and not necessarily reliable for optimal investment decisions. The fact that fund managers are aware of such biases, however, suggests that they treat the information from analysts (especially share recommendations) with a degree of scepticism. These findings are also in accordance with Dugar and Nathan (1995), who, in a domestic setting and using a market-based research design, concluded that investors appear to be aware of analysts' potential conflicts of interest and consequently rely more on analysts without investment banker relationships to form future expectations of company performance.

8.6.2 Regional variation

Figure 8.1 represents the overall information flows between analysts and fund managers in transnational analysis. However, reliance on foreign analysts and local research varied within and between geographic regions, particularly for European, Asian (excluding Japan) and South American companies. In these regions, foreign analysts were typically based in a 'hub' of a geographical region, where analysts for a number of different countries are based in a major financial centre. For South American countries, analysts are based primarily in New York, whereas outside Tokyo, Singapore and Hong Kong are the two main centres in Asia. For European companies, analysts are based increasingly in London, from where pan European research is conducted (thus, all of the sell-side analysts interviewed in the current research were European specialists based in London).

This helps to explain the questionnaire results in Table 7.5, which show that relative to UK fund managers, who cover companies globally, UK analysts are more focused on European companies. London and the UK are thus European hubs for sell-side analysis, but globally orientated in fund management. Despite this, in Europe, some analytical research still takes place locally. One analyst commented that this research was sometimes superior to that from London based analysts:

> Where a company is European and has offices across the community, the best information and the best analysis is done in the local sector, and that springs from the fact that they do understand the accounting standards in full, they do understand the culture, and they understand the language. (Analyst 2)

Furthermore, Analyst 1 (a European construction companies analyst based in London) and Analyst 3 (a European telecoms companies analyst based in London) both acknowledged that they occasionally rely on local analysts for certain countries.

8.7 DISCUSSION AND CONCLUSIONS

All the evidence in this chapter points to direct company contact and the annual report being the most useful information sources to both analysts and fund managers involved in transnational analysis. Despite some indications from the literature that the annual report would be relatively more useful in domestic versus transnational analysis, the questionnaire results fail to support this. Indeed, in some cases (i.e., previous annual report and preliminary announcements) accounting information is significantly more useful in transnational analysis than in domestic analysis.

In common with findings of research into domestic analysis, the annual report is a vital reference document, and also informs and provides a basis for fund managers' meetings with management. For analysts, the annual report is a key information source in their detailed analysis, forming a central basis for earnings forecasts and for confirming their own research. In transnational analysis, the annual report also plays an important confirmatory role, as it is used by fund managers to verify management disclosures and analysts' research. Thus, while the annual report may not be a timely document, it is nevertheless relied upon as a dependable, comprehensive information source in an investment environment characterised by heightened uncertainty.

The results relating to the Securities and Exchange Companies (SEC) Form 20-F indicate that for non-US companies, there is scope for improvement in the information disclosed in the annual report. Although it is only available for companies with a US listing, Form 20-F is considered very useful in transnational analysis. Analysts and fund managers held this additional disclosure in high regard, especially as it contains incremental disclosure to annual reports. This is consistent with prior market-based research which demonstrates that 20-F disclosures contain incremental information to national disclosures (e.g., Barth and Clinch, 1996). However, most prior research assumes that this information is as a result of US GAAP (i.e., an accounting measurement issue), whereas the results of the interviews in the current research indicate that it is also a product of higher disclosure quality. An interesting question is whether this result holds after the accounting problems surrounding the recent large scale US corporate collapses of Enron and WorldCom.

Information direct from the company either in personal form such as company meetings and presentations, or in published form (particularly the annual report) is highly valued by analysts and fund managers. However, the role and significance of company management in transnational analysis cannot be considered in isolation. Importantly, from a UK perspective, overseas company management as a source of information should be seen alongside locally-based sell-side analysts, who are vitally important in transnational analysis. This is because local analysts represent an interface between UK fund managers and overseas company management. In this capacity, analysts based in the region or country where the subject company is domiciled are able to mitigate or eliminate many of the obstacles faced by foreign investors. They represent a first point of contact for UK fund managers and, in addition to being providers of information, research and analysis themselves, local analysts perform the important function of providing ongoing access to overseas management. This access may be in the local country or, with the assistance of the analysts' firm, in the UK. An exception to this is that for European companies, UK-based analysts are most useful. This is perhaps due to the increasing tendency for UK analysts to specialise by sector across the European region, as described in Chapter 7.

The perceived usefulness of overseas analysts would suggest that analyst following of foreign companies is associated with levels of transnational investment. A recent working paper by Aggarwal *et al.* (2004) offers support for this in an investigation of determinants of investment in overseas firms by US mutual funds. They find that analyst following is a significant firm-level determinant of foreign investment, even after controlling for factors such as accounting and stock-market performance, firm size and accounting quality. That is, the greater the number of analysts following a firm, the more likely US mutual funds are to invest in that firm.

One final point to note on the use of the annual report in transnational analysis is the potential barrier of language differences. Clearly, this barrier is not sufficient to prevent the use of the annual report. This is partly due to the availability of English language versions of the annual report. This raises questions about whether fund managers avoid companies which only provide foreign language annual reports. Further research will be necessary to examine whether such companies receive less attention than those which publish English translations, and whether there are any economic implications arising from this, such as effects on the cost of capital for these companies.

Interestingly, the balance sheet is ranked as the most useful component of transnational annual reports. Although consideration of balance sheet characteristics is important in domestic analysis, certain reasons for a focus on the balance sheet are more important in transnational analysis. Financing and ownership information was considered particularly relevant by the interviewees. Levels of debt may assume a greater significance given the additional risk introduced by foreign currency volatility. This result is in line with the findings of Kang and Stulz (1997) who found that debt levels are negatively associated with foreign ownership of Japanese shares. Details of minority interests are also relevant for gauging attitudes to outside shareholders. Furthermore, cash flow information is either scarce, or not readily available in a suitable format in some foreign companies' annual reports. This finding offers a potential explanation for the relative positions of the cash flow statement and balance sheet in domestic versus transnational analysis in this questionnaire survey. Overall, in domestic analysis, the cash flow statement is the most useful component of the annual report, followed by the balance sheet. In transnational analysis, however, these results are reversed. As such, the balance sheet is fulfilling its role as a primary information source in itself, while simultaneously providing supplementary information for the derivation of an appropriate, reliable cash flow measure.

Increased focus on the balance sheet is also a product of an approach in transnational investment, where company security and stability assume a greater significance than in domestic analysis. Information asymmetries are a likely contributory factor to this result. Gehrig (1993) *inter alia* states that, on average, investors are better informed about domestic equities than foreign equities. It is unsurprising then that transnational investors impose high hurdles in terms of the integrity of the investment as a compensatory allowance for the risk that their information set is inadequate. This is not to say that balance sheet security is the only important factor in transnational investment decisions. Rather, as noted in the interviews, the importance of sound balance sheet characteristics is augmented by national boundaries and the associated disparities in information access. Previts *et al.* (1994) also found that for poorly understood companies, analysts focused more on balance sheet factors. To the extent that UK analysts and investors understand overseas companies less than UK companies, this ties in with the findings of the current research.

In sum, this chapter demonstrates that despite geographical and logistical barriers, direct contact with companies and management still forms an integral part of the decision-making information set to analysts and fund managers. Moreover, reliance on accounting information, especially the annual report, is apparently not materially affected by the presence of national boundaries; both analysts and fund managers find such information very useful in the analysis of domestic and overseas equities. Finally, such sources are not used in isolation; locally-based analysts are often viewed as an important interface between UK-based fund managers and overseas companies. However, the limitations of analysts' advice have not gone unnoticed by the UK investment community.

8.8 REFERENCES

Aggarwal, R., Klapper, L. and Wysocki, P.D. (2004). 'Portfolio preferences of foreign institutional investors.' *MIT Sloan School of Management Working Paper*.

Barker, R.G. (1998). 'The market for information: evidence from finance directors, analysts and fund managers.' *Accounting and Business Research*, **29** (1), 1–20.

Barker, R.G. (2001). *Institutional Investors, Accounting Information and the ASB*. Institute of Charted Accountants of Scotland, Edinburgh.

Barth, M.E. and Clinch, G. (1996). 'International accounting differences and their relation to share prices: evidence from UK, Australian and Canadian Firms.' *Contemporary Accounting Research*, **13** (1), 135–170.

Dugar, A. and Nathan, S. (1995). 'The effect of investment banking relationships on financial analysts' earnings forecasts and investment recommendations.' *Contemporary Accounting Research*, **12** (1), 131–160.

Gehrig, T. (1993). 'An information based explanation of the domestic bias in international equity investment.' *Scandinavian Journal of Economics*, **95** (1), 97–109.

Holland, J. (1998). 'Private disclosure and financial reporting.' *Accounting and Business Research*, **28** (4), 255–269.

Kang, J. and Stulz, R.M. (1997). 'Why is there a home-bias? An analysis of foreign portfolio equity ownership in Japan.' *Journal of Financial Economics*, **46**, 3–28.

Moizer, P. and Arnold, J. (1984). 'Share appraisal by investment analysts – portfolio vs. non-portfolio managers.' *Accounting and Business Research*, **Autumn**, 341–348.

Previts, G.J., Bricker, R.J., Robinson, T.R. and Young, S.J. (1994). 'A content analysis of sell-side analyst company reports.' *Accounting Horizons*, **8** (2), 55–70.

9
Views of International Accounting Diversity and Harmonisation

9.1 INTRODUCTION

At first sight, transnational investors can be seen as obvious supporters of the harmonisation of international accounting standards. Much independent academic work and policy pronouncements of the International Accounting Standards Board (IASB) assume this stance. However, this view is predicated on two assumptions. First, that accounting information is of sufficient importance in transnational analysis to warrant support for (or indeed, any interest in) harmonisation. Second, even if the first assumption holds, sophisticated users of transnational accounting information must consider the benefits of harmonisation to outweigh the costs. Such costs include, *inter alia*, the erosion of the comparative advantage analysts and fund managers possess in interpreting and analysing transnational accounting information.

The results in Chapter 8 demonstrate that the first assumption appears to be valid – accounting information, particularly the financial statements, is of primary importance in the analysis of overseas equities. This chapter aims to examine the validity of the second assumption. The first section examines how analysts and fund managers perceive their transnational decision making to be affected by international accounting differences. The second section examines the views of analysts and fund managers on the international harmonisation of accounting standards and demonstrates strong support for harmonisation among the financial community.

9.2 THE EFFECTS OF INTERNATIONAL ACCOUNTING DIFFERENCES ON INVESTMENT DECISIONS

The research reviewed in Chapter 3 demonstrated that significant international diversity exists in accounting measurement and disclosure standards. Given these differences, and the fact that accounting information is highly

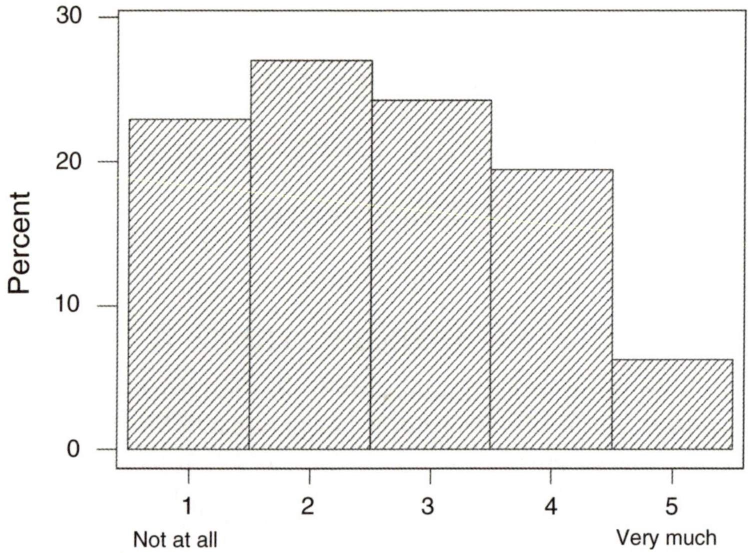

Figure 9.1 International accounting differences affect decisions

important in transnational equity analysis, it would be reasonable to predict that fund managers and analysts perceive their decisions to be affected by international accounting differences. It was also noted in Chapter 3 that what limited prior research there is into the effects of international accounting differences offers little in the way of consensus, other than some analysts and fund managers feel that their decisions are affected by international accounting differences, while others do not.

To directly investigate the effects of international accounting diversity, analysts and fund managers involved in foreign company analysis were asked in the questionnaire to what extent differences in international accounting affect their decision making. Respondents were requested to answer on a five-point scale, where 1 = not at all, and 5 = very much.

Figure 9.1 presents the frequencies of the responses to this question from the overall sample. The responses are skewed towards the lower end of the scale, consistent with respondents' decisions not being affected by international accounting differences. Only nine analysts and fund managers (6.3%) stated that international accounting differences affected their decision making very much, whereas 33 respondents (23%) said that accounting differences had no impact at all on their decisions. The mean response on the five-point scale was 2.59 – significantly lower than the mid point of 3.

Table 9.1 Views of analysts and fund managers on the effects of accounting diversity

	Fund managers		Investment analysts		Total	
	Mean	Std. Dev	Mean	Std. dev	Mean	Std. dev
Accounting differences affect decisions (1 = not at all; 5 = very much)	2.64	1.26	2.49	1.12	2.59	1.21

9.2.1 Differences between analysts and fund managers

International accounting differences may be expected to be more problematic for fund managers than analysts for a number of reasons. First, as shown in Chapter 7, analysts follow fewer companies and are also likely to conduct fewer international comparisons than fund managers. In addition, because analysts do not have to construct and monitor portfolios, they are able to conduct more detailed analysis of company information, and are more likely to be familiar with the intricacies of international accounting systems.

The higher mean response of fund managers shown in Table 9.1 is consistent with this prediction (2.64 versus 2.49). Furthermore, and as shown in Table 9.2, whereas only one analyst (2%) indicated that international accounting differences affected his decisions very much, eight fund managers (8%) felt very much affected by international accounting differences.

However, the difference between the two groups is marginal and a Mann-Whitney test showed that it was not statistically significant. The evidence therefore suggests that overall, analysts and fund managers do not perceive differences in international accounting systems to have a significant effect on their decision making.

Table 9.2 Effects of international accounting diversity

	Not at all affected 1		2		3		4		Very much affected 5	
	n	%	n	%	n	%	n	%	n	%
Fund managers	23	23.2	25	25.3	24	22.2	19	19.2	8	8.1
Analysts	10	22.2	14	31.1	11	24.4	9	20.0	1	2.2

A potential factor to consider when investigating this issue in this way is the possibility that fund managers and analysts say they are not affected by international accounting differences because they have adopted coping strategies or adjusted their appraisal techniques *because of* international accounting differences. For example, in the interviews, Analyst 7 noted that the institution which employed him modified its discounted cash flow model to take account of international differences in accounting for depreciation, provisions and extraordinary items; although his response on the five-point scale indicated that he was not at all affected by international accounting differences. The results of the questionnaire should therefore be interpreted with this in mind.

In accordance with Miles and Nobes (1998), who found that country specialists were less affected by international accounting differences than sector specialists, the sample was split into those who specialised by country or geographic region and those who did not. The results indicated that region specialists are less affected by international accounting differences (means of 2.84 and 2.52 for non specialists and specialists respectively), but the difference was not statistically significant. The lack of significant difference may be because geographic specialism can mean that analysts and fund managers cover diverse countries within the region in which they specialise. For example, European, Asian and emerging market specialists will still encounter substantial intra-regional accounting diversity.

9.2.2 International variation in the effects of international accounting differences

The results in Chapters 7 and 8 indicated that the usefulness of information sources and appraisal techniques is partially contingent upon the country of the company being analysed. There was some evidence that the effects of international accounting differences were also country-dependent in the interviews; virtually all respondents stated that the quality of accounting information disclosed by companies varies by country or by geographic region. Germany, Switzerland and Japan were the countries most frequently mentioned as being problematic. These three countries were also singled out in the Choi and Levich (1991) study as being a source of concern for analysts when investing abroad.

In the case of Japan, poor disclosure of cash flow, pension liabilities and company ownership data were the main areas of accounting disclosure deficiencies. Japanese accounting measurement principles were also criticised by numerous fund managers and analysts. Specific areas mentioned were out of date fixed asset values, lack of consolidation and off-balance sheet financing. However, recent changes in Japanese accounting standards mean that some of these issues (particularly consolidated financial statements) are now less problematic (Seki, 2000).

Somewhat unsurprisingly, the most severe problems with accounting standards were encountered by fund managers who were responsible for portfolios of companies from emerging markets. Both measurement and disclosure standards were often viewed as problematic. Fund Manager 10 was originally an analyst of US companies, but is now a senior emerging markets analyst. He noted that:

> After working in US markets, [the difference in disclosure] is particularly noticeable – from getting quarterly financial statements days after the period to getting three pieces of paper at the year end if you are lucky! You therefore have to try and rely more on that subjective part of the analysis where you are working on countries that do not have decent accounting information; in developed markets, disciplined systems are used with investment rules and financial models. In emerging markets you probably invest across more companies than you would normally do and you should diversify out of sectors because there may be accounting irregularity across the whole sector.

Despite their concerns in this context, most analysts and fund managers stated that in general, the quality of disclosure is improving over time. Furthermore, there was widespread acknowledgement that the 'country effect' was not the only determinant of disclosure quality; size and maturity of the company being the additional key factors mentioned.

9.2.3 Accounting standards and the cost of capital

One of the open ended sections of the questionnaire asked analysts and fund managers what they regarded as the additional costs (if any) of dealing with international accounting differences. Comments on a number of questionnaires indicated that companies reporting figures under non-IAS/US GAAP were categorised as higher risk.[1] Therefore, in the interviews, respondents were asked whether they agreed with this, and to elaborate further on this issue. Many respondents revealed a certain reluctance to invest in companies not reporting under IAS and US GAAP and both analysts and fund managers referred to a 'quality effect' added by recognised accounting standards. Specifically, standards such as IAS or US GAAP were often perceived to lead to improvements on local standards in respect of both measurement and disclosure of accounting information. Additionally, recognisable standards were sometimes seen as a 'stamp of approval' for the accounts, and

[1] In this context, reference to overseas companies reporting under US GAAP excludes US companies.

as a signal of managements' attitudes towards shareholders. This applied both to developing markets and to developed markets, including Japan and Western Europe. The following quote is illustrative:

> Using recognised accounting standards can give companies a better, broader, more international fundamental shareholder base. It shows a will to try and disclose information and to suggest some kind of shareholder friendly behaviour, and wanting to give shareholders some information, and that is a good step for Europe, whether it is IAS or US GAAP. (Fund Manager 7).

A consequence of this is that risk premia are attached to the securities of these companies by analysts and fund managers, effectively translating into a relationship between the accounting standards used and the cost of capital through a higher discount rate. This viewpoint was summed up by Analyst 7:

> Companies in Europe who move to IAS or US GAAP have a premium attached to their share price. I have seen that happen where the share price moves up on the announcement that they were changing accounting standards.

A similar phenomenon was mentioned in Marton (1998), who noted that this additional premium was required to take account of additional 'accounting risk'. Interestingly, part of the responsibility for this was attributed to the reluctance of US investors to invest in companies with accounting standards which are unfamiliar to them. Given the significance of the funds available for investment in the US,[2] and the home bias documented in previous literature, where US investors hold excessive levels of domestic shares in their portfolios, this appears highly plausible. As noted by Fund Managers 10 and 12:

> If you want to attract investors, then use the standard that those investors are familiar with. You need to make the job easier for fund managers and analysts to get them to invest in your company. (Fund Manager 10)

> As a financial manager who invests on the basis of fundamentals, the less risk there is associated with the balance sheet and earnings in terms of prediction risk, the higher the price. You have to apply a discount for all the 'nasties' that might be there that you can't see. (Fund Manager 12)

Although there was widespread agreement that a premium exists on the shares which report under more familiar accounting standards, many fund managers and analysts acknowledged that this premium may also be attributable to other factors. In particular, non-US companies that report under US GAAP are generally US listed, which brings other significant benefits. As discussed in Chapter 2, US markets are characterised by high liquidity,

[2] US institutional investors' financial assets in 1998 were US$18,005 million (OECD, 2000).

and US listings result in high firm visibility. Furthermore, many companies reporting under US GAAP are successful multinational firms whose higher share price (resulting from a lower discount rate) may also be attributable to sound fundamentals, in addition to their use of recognisable accounting standards for their financial statements.

These findings are, however, consistent with the literature that demonstrates a link between disclosure and the cost of equity capital (Botosan, 1997; Leuz and Verrecchia, 2000). They are also supported by the results of Aggrawal *et al.* (2004), who found that investment in overseas firms by US mutual funds is positively related to whether the firm complies with US GAAP/IAS in preparing its financial statements, and to the quality of the firm's disclosure.

In sum, the results of this section are consistent with analysts' and fund managers' decisions not being materially affected by international accounting differences, although this depends, at least in part, on where the company being analysed is based. Moreover, and in line with Choi and Levich (1991), fund managers and analysts have developed ways of coping with international accounting differences. The following section examines the related issue of analysts' and fund managers' levels of support for the harmonisation of international accounting standards.

9.3 VIEWS ON THE INTERNATIONAL HARMONISATION OF ACCOUNTING

It was pointed out in Chapter 3 that although there has been very little empirical evidence on the issue, there are principally two opposing views on whether analysts and fund managers support moves to reduce international accounting diversity through harmonisation. The first view is that, largely due to the lack of comparability of financial statements internationally, institutional users of accounting information view harmonisation positively as it will facilitate easier cross-border comparisons (e.g., Cairns, 1994; Roach, 1996; Nobes, 2002). The second is that, for various reasons, analysts and fund managers do not view harmonisation as a positive process. Such reasons include self-interest arguments surrounding the potential erosion of analysts' comparative advantage in international financial analysis and advice (e.g., Hopwood, 1994); or international accounting differences not being of sufficient import to warrant harmonisation (e.g., Goeltz, 1991); and finally, harmonisation not being appropriate due to the inherent diversity in national accounting systems (e.g., Ball, 1995). Respondents were therefore asked for their views on harmonisation in the questionnaire survey and in the interviews.

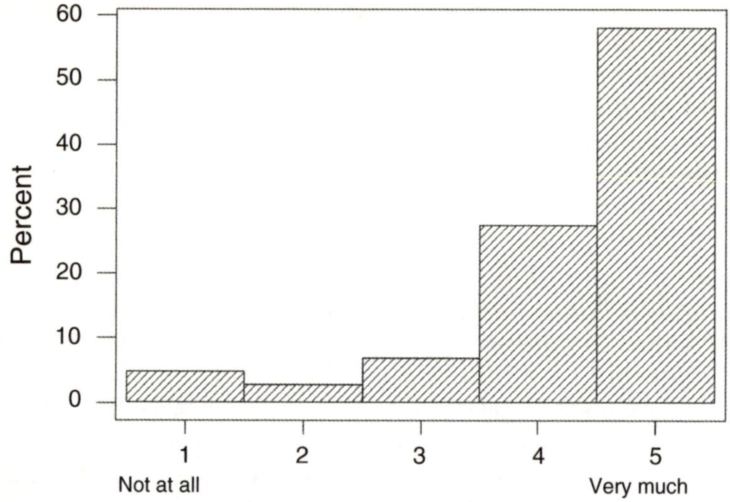

Figure 9.2 Would like to see accounting standards harmonised

In the questionnaire survey, respondents were asked to what extent they would like to see international accounting diversity reduced via harmonisation. A five-point scale was used, where 1 = not at all and 5 = very much. A histogram of responses from the overall sample is presented in Figure 9.2.

The distribution is heavily skewed towards the higher end on the scale, indicating that across the whole sample of analysts and fund managers, there is widespread support for harmonisation: 58% of analysts and fund managers are 'very much' in favour of harmonisation, whereas only 4.8% are 'not at all' in favour.

In line with these questionnaire findings, there was widespread support for the harmonisation process in the interviews. Of all 31 respondents, 29 were supportive of harmonisation[3] and not one of the respondents took a negative view of harmonisation. The support was often emphatic. For example, Analyst 1 commented:

> I'm delighted for [accounting standards] to be harmonised – irrespective of the way in which they are harmonised. I have a view perhaps of what I think is the right way to treat things, but I don't mind so much what conclusion they come to, so long as they come to one.

However, some analysts and fund managers did not want harmonisation at any price and a number of reservations were expressed about the

[3] The remaining two did not give direct responses to the question, i.e., when asked for their views on harmonisation, they did not say explicitly whether they were in favour or against it.

Table 9.3 Preferences for IAS and US GAAP

	Fund Managers				
	No response	Local standards	IAS	US GAAP	No preference
Number	5	0	2	2	11
%	25	0	10	10	55
	Analysts				
	No response	Local standards	IAS	US GAAP	No preference
Number	2	0	0	2	7
%	18	0	0	18	64
	Total				
	No response	Local standards	IAS	US GAAP	No preference
Number	7	0	2	4	18
%	23	0	6	13	58

harmonisation process. Fund Manager 11 voiced concerns about accounting standards being forced to the 'lowest common denominator', while Fund Manager 18 worried that there is insufficient scrutiny of standards such as IAS and US GAAP by practitioners.

Overall, analysts and fund managers expressed little preference between IAS and US GAAP standards. This was seen as a subsidiary issue to the harmonisation question itself. More specifically, analysts and fund managers were asked about their preference for companies' use of local standards, IAS, or US GAAP. The results are presented in Table 9.3.

As the results show, very few fund managers (11 out of 14 who responded) or analysts (7 out of 9 who responded) expressed a preference for either IAS or US GAAP. Furthermore, of the 4 respondents who expressed a preference for US GAAP, 3 stated that they did not have strong views over which were used. The remaining respondent was a manager of a US fund, so it is unsurprising that he preferred US GAAP because of his experience with these standards. This indifference between the two sets of standards is consistent with Leuz (2003) who, in a market-based study of the German 'New Market', found no significant differences in the informational qualities of IAS and US GAAP. However, it could be conjectured that analysts' and fund managers' views have changed since the survey was conducted, following the Enron and WorldCom cases in the US, which brought into question the integrity of US GAAP.

In line with the research outlined in Chapter 3, there was little interest among analysts and fund managers in the political aspects of the harmonisation debate. Two exceptions were Fund Manager 13, who expressed reservations over wholesale adoption of US GAAP and Analyst 9 who was concerned about excessive US influence in the harmonisation process. A European sell-side analyst (Analyst 1) summed up the consensus opinion:

> Analysts are keen to have a solution, whereas people involved in preparing the accounts themselves are keen to have a solution that suits what they think. We are agnostic about the solution – we want a decision. We are a step back from that – less involved in the politics of it.

Overall, these results emphasise that although analysts and investors may be reluctant to become involved in the politics of the harmonisation process (see also Hopwood (1994) and Kenny and Larson (1995) discussed in Chapter 3), it should not automatically be inferred that they have no interest in harmonisation itself.

9.3.1 Differences between analysts and fund managers

Due to the possibility that fund managers become less reliant upon analysts for the analysis of foreign companies following the harmonisation of accounting standards, analysts might reasonably be expected to be less supportive of harmonisation. However, this hypothesis is not supported by the mean responses presented in Table 9.4, as the difference between analysts and fund managers (4.34 versus 4.26) is only marginal. Indeed, despite having potential motivations for preserving the status quo, the results in Table 9.4 show that analysts remain highly supportive of the harmonisation of international accounting standards.

Further support for the notion that investment analysts are in favour of harmonisation is provided by analysis of the frequency of responses to the harmonisation question in Table 9.5: 60% of analysts were 'very much' in favour of harmonisation, whereas only 6% indicated that they would

Table 9.4 Views of analysts and fund managers on harmonisation

	Fund managers		Investment analysts		Total	
	Mean	Std. dev	Mean	Std. dev	Mean	Std. dev
Would like to see harmonisation	4.34	0.99	4.26	1.17	4.32	1.04

Table 9.5 Views of international harmonisation of accounting standards

	Would like to see harmonisation									
	Not at all 1		2		3		4		Very much 5	
	n	%	n	%	n	%	n	%	n	%
Fund managers	4	4.0	2	2.0	7	7.1	29	29.3	57	57.6
Analysts	3	6.4	2	4.3	3	6.4	11	23.4	28	59.6

not like to see accounting standards harmonised at all. Similarly, all the analysts in the interviews were favourably disposed towards harmonisation. There is therefore no evidence that fund managers are more supportive of harmonisation than investment analysts.

9.3.2 Reasons for support for harmonisation

Previous research frequently cites the importance of comparable accounting information to the financial community as a primary driver of the harmonisation of international accounting standards. Views of analysts and fund managers were therefore sought to ascertain how important the comparability of accounting information is in transnational investment.[4]

In the interviews, it was generally acknowledged that comparability of financial statements is highly important. However, the concerns over comparability were voiced more by fund managers than by investment analysts. This reflects the more specialist nature of analysts compared to fund managers, as discussed in previous chapters. It is also in line with the significantly greater number of companies that fund managers cover, shown in Table 7.4. Analyst 2, for example, stated:

> There is no difficulty in making comparisons at the level you want to make them at, and investors don't have any problem interpreting that information either.

Support from investment analysts for harmonisation was based more upon the costs of increased familiarity with (sometimes multiple) foreign accounting standards:[5]

[4] Following Miles and Nobes (1998) tests were also conducted between country specialists and industry specialists' views of harmonisation, and of the impact of international accounting differences. No differences were found between these two groups.

[5] Although one fund manager also quoted the time spent understanding foreign accounting information as a cost of transnational analysis.

> If you look at an investor investing, or thinking of investing say in Africa, if he has to go through about 2 weeks of learning the accounting standards of the country, he will probably never make a return on it. But because he knows the standards, he can look at it and say 'OK, these are the reported numbers under the standards I know', the investment decision can be made much quicker and the investor feels much safer. (Analyst 3)

9.4 DISCUSSION AND CONCLUSIONS

As discussed in Chapter 3, despite assumptions of unqualified support dominating the international accounting harmonisation debate, theoretical and pragmatic reasons exist for fund managers and analysts to resist moves towards harmonised international accounting standards. On the other hand, the argument that international accounting differences are a hindrance to financial statement users would suggest widespread support for the harmonisation of international accounting standards. In an attempt to address the point made by Hopwood (1994) that arguments in this area have been based largely on conjecture and assumptions and not on empirical evidence, this chapter presents the results of the questionnaire and interview surveys. These results suggest that fund managers and analysts do not perceive their decisions to be significantly affected by international accounting differences. In line with the findings of Marton (1998), the results also confirm strong support for harmonisation across the transnational financial community.

The increased inconvenience caused by non-comparable accounting information appears to precipitate stronger feelings towards harmonisation. Discussions in the interviews confirmed the importance of comparability, particularly for fund managers. Importantly, however, comparability of accounting information is not the only issue determining support for harmonisation. Transnational analysts and fund managers are also concerned about the quality of measurement and disclosure in some national financial reporting systems.

A further interesting finding from this research is that investors and analysts attach a risk premium to the securities of companies which do not report under widely accepted and reputable accounting standards. Thus, shares of overseas companies which do not use IAS or US GAAP are, *ceteris paribus,* valued using a higher discount rate. The implications of this are wide ranging, especially for the harmonisation debate. Essentially, this represents a market-based mechanism to encourage companies to use common accounting standards. The IASB, therefore, can be seen as an organisation which is facilitating harmonisation by establishing a suitable set of accounting standards without the political difficulty of having a particular nationality attached to them. However, the market holds the ultimate sanction over companies, by penalising companies that do not use standards which are familiar and trusted by capital providers. Therefore, if companies wish to raise capital at the lowest cost, they need to use standards familiar to the main international capital providers. Furthermore, this result may imply a superior ability of investors with in-depth knowledge of local accounting standards in certain countries to discriminate between investment opportunities; this is an issue worthy of future research.

This finding also has important implications for the specific issue of IAS enforcement in the harmonisation debate. The limited enforcement capabilities of the IASB's predecessor, the IASC, have often been seen as an impediment to the widespread adoption of IAS. However, if the IASB is seen as a *facilitator* rather than as an *enforcer* of harmonisation, punitive action can be left to the market which will discourage, through the imposition of risk premia, the use of unreliable or opaque accounting standards, thus encouraging the use of IAS. This does raise the interesting question of whether, even if, according to some objective criteria, there were no differences between non-UK countries' standards and IAS or US GAAP in the quality of accounting measurement and disclosure, there will still remain a 'residual' difference in the perceptions of UK analysts and fund managers. That is, is the extra confidence afforded to IAS and US GAAP by UK financial institutions justified? This is also a question worthy of future research.

The next chapter concludes the book with a summary of the research and a discussion of the limitations and implications of the findings.

9.5 REFERENCES

Aggarwal, R., Klapper, L. and Wysocki, P.D. (2004). 'Portfolio preferences of foreign institutional investors.' *MIT Sloan School of Management Working Paper*.

Ball, R. (1995). 'Making accounting more international: why, how and how far will it go?' *Journal of Applied Corporate Finance*, **8** (3), 19–29.

Botosan, C.A. (1997). 'Disclosure level and the cost of equity capital.' *The Accounting Review*, **72** (3), 323–349.

Cairns, D. (1994). 'What is the future of mutual recognition of financial statements and is comparability really necessary?' *The European Accounting Review*, **3** (2), 343–352.

Choi, F.D.S. and Levich, R.M. (1991). 'Behavioral effects of international accounting diversity.' *Accounting Horizons*, **June**, 1–13.

Goeltz, R.K. (1991). 'International accounting harmonisation: the impossible (and unnecessary?) dream.' *Accounting Horizons*, **March**, 85–88.

Hopwood, A.G. (1994). 'Some reflections on "The Harmonization of Accounting Within the EU".' *The European Accounting Review*, **3** (2), 241–253.

Kenny, S.Y. and Larson, R.K. (1995). 'The development of international accounting standards: an analysis of constituent participation in standards setting.' *International Journal of Accounting*, **30**, 283–301.

Leuz, C. (2003). 'IAS versus US GAAP: information-asymmetry based evidence from Germany's new market.' *Journal of Accounting Research*, **41**, 445–472.

Leuz, C. and Verrecchia, R.E. (2000). 'The economic consequences of increased disclosure.' *Journal of Accounting Research*, **38**, 91–124.

Marton, J. (1998). *Accounting and Stock Markets: A Study of Swedish Accounting for International Investors and Analysts*, BAS, Gothenburg University, Sweden.

Miles, S. and Nobes, C. (1998). 'The use of foreign accounting data in UK financial institutions.' *Journal of Business Finance and Accounting*, **25** (3 and 4), 309–328.

Nobes, C.W. (2002). 'International harmonisation of accounting.' In Nobes, C.W. and Parker, R.H. *Comparative International* Accounting, 7th edn, Pearson Education, Harlow.

OECD (2000). *Institutional Investors Statistical Yearbook*, Organization for Economic Co-operation and Development, Paris.

Roach, N. (1996). 'Global accounting standards: an investor's view.' *Journal of International Financial Management and Accounting*, **7** (1), 74–81.

Seki, M. (2000). 'Reshaping standards.' *Accountancy*, **June**, 110.

10

Overview and Conclusions

This chapter concludes the book with a discussion of the previous chapters and their implications. The next section summarises the motivation for the book. The key findings are then discussed, along with the implications and limitations of the empirical study. The final section offers some concluding remarks.

10.1 MOTIVATION FOR THE BOOK

To date, and in spite of the enormous growth in overseas equity transactions over recent decades, there has been little examination of the processes and techniques involved in transnational equity decision making. Moreover, the extant literature on cross-border decision making has investigated the use of accounting information, but has largely neglected the role of other information sources. This book has aimed to go some way to address this lack of research.

Knowledge of the processes involved in cross-border decision making is important in order to understand overseas capital allocation. Relatively little is known about how international differences in accounting and financial reporting affect transnational equity decisions. Research in this area is also necessary to fully inform the debate on the harmonisation of international accounting. The International Accounting Standards Board (IASB) is striving for a unified set of accounting and financial reporting standards which is acceptable to global stock markets and investors. Prior research is largely based on assumptions of support for harmonisation due to negative effects of international accounting diversity. However, there is little empirical evidence to support this (Hopwood, 1994).

Previous investigations of domestic equity analysis (i.e., where the investor is located in the same country as the investee company) have yielded remarkably consistent results, showing that fundamental analysis is the predominant appraisal technique. Accordingly, accounting information and direct company contact play a critical role in informing these investment decisions. However, the findings of domestic research are not necessarily applicable to transnational decision making due to international differences in financial reporting systems. In addition, the usefulness of transnational analysis techniques and information sources may vary *between* different countries. The comparative international accounting literature discussed in Chapter 3 demonstrates that in certain countries, financial reporting systems are not orientated towards equity users, which may militate against the usefulness of reported accounting figures and other management disclosures.

In order to investigate these issues, a survey of analysts and fund managers was conducted. As noted in the introduction, in broad terms, the objectives of the research were:

(i) to examine the relative usefulness of the various analysis techniques used in transnational equity investment decisions;
(ii) to investigate the utility of accounting information and other information sources in transnational equity analysis;
(iii) to assess the impact of international accounting differences on fund managers' and analysts' decision making; and
(iv) to examine the views of analysts and fund managers who are engaged in transnational equity analysis on the international harmonisation of accounting standards.

10.2 SUMMARY OF FINDINGS AND IMPLICATIONS

10.2.1 Equity analysis techniques

In line with the findings of previous studies into domestic equity analysis, the results of the current research show an overwhelming preference for fundamental analysis in the analysis of UK equities. More importantly, however, this result also holds for transnational equity analysis – fundamental analysis is regarded as the most useful technique by fund managers and analysts when analysing overseas shares. Therefore, international accounting differences do not appear to deter analysts and fund managers from using techniques that involve the analysis of financial statements. There are, however, some differences within the fundamental approach. The survey indicated that when analysing overseas companies, fund managers and analysts use modified earnings measures which exclude some accounting accruals. In particular, earnings before interest, taxation, depreciation and amortisation (EBITDA) is considered a useful measure for international comparisons of accounting information because it mitigates many effects of international accounting differences. This measure makes comparisons easier by 'moving up' the income statement and avoiding many areas of accounting susceptible to international variation.

What is unclear is whether moving up the income statement results in important and relevant information being lost, and whether this leads to suboptimal investment decisions. There is some evidence that accruals information (most of which is lost in using EBITDA) is value relevant (Charitou and Edwards, 1990). Additionally, research by Francis *et al.* (2003) in the US demonstrates that comprehensive earnings measures (which include items such as depreciation, interest and taxation) are more closely associated with share returns than EBITDA, at least in domestic equity analysis.

In response to the lack of comparability and possible unfamiliarity with international financial reporting systems, fund managers and analysts may be expected to place more emphasis on non-accounting analysis techniques (such as technical analysis and top-down analysis), as they rely on market-based information rather than accounting inputs. However, fund managers and analysts do not subordinate fundamental analysis to non-accounting techniques in the analysis of foreign equities. In fact, the results indicate that technical analysis is more useful in the analysis of UK shares than in transnational analysis. In line with Olbert (1994), this result appears to be attributable to the fact that technical analysis is more useful in more developed and more liquid stock markets.

There is little evidence of any significant international variation in the use of transnational analysis techniques: fundamental analysis is the most prevalent, irrespective of the country of origin of the investee company. However, top-down analysis and discounted cash flow techniques are regarded as more useful in emerging markets and in Asia than in other regions, possibly due to poor accounting disclosures. Differences between analysts and fund managers were also investigated. The results showed that although analysts and fund managers use the same techniques, fund managers attach greater significance to technical analysis than investment analysts. This technique is used for timing transnational investment decisions, rather than for determining in which companies to invest; however, relative to fundamental analysis, technical analysis is not highly regarded.

10.2.2 Transnational information sources

Also in line with the literature on domestic equity analysis, accounting information and the annual report are essential sources of information in transnational equity analysis, particularly to investment analysts. Apart from direct company contact, the annual report is the most influential source of information on foreign companies. UK-based analysts and fund managers are heavily dependent on English translations of the annual report, and make limited use of original foreign language versions. As with UK company analysis, the annual report serves as an agenda-setting device for management meetings. It acts as a prompt for further questioning of management and is seen as a reliable, verifiable benchmark information source.

The financial statements form an integral part of transnational analysis, despite international accounting differences. They are the most influential part of the annual report, although narrative information is more useful in the analysis of foreign firms than in UK company analysis. Interestingly, the balance sheet is considered very useful in the analysis of overseas firms – it is used to ensure investment security and liquidity, and to assess debt levels. Such issues concerning company stability and risk appear to be particularly important in transnational analysis. In addition, the balance sheet is sometimes used as a device to supplement transnational cash flow information, which is not always available, or is often in an unsuitable format. This increased focus on the balance sheet relative to the income statement corresponds with the position of UK Accounting Standards Board, the IASB, and the US Financial Accounting Standards Board (Davies *et al*., 1999), although it is inconsistent with recent empirical research into UK equity analysis (Barker, 2001).

Direct personal contact through company visits and meetings with management proved to be the most influential source to both investment analysts and fund managers. Such information is considered vital both for domestic, and perhaps more surprisingly, for overseas company analysis. Indeed, most fund managers would not consider investment in overseas companies unless they had had some personal contact with company management. These meetings are used to acquire financial information for investment decisions, and also to establish personal relationships with company management. Analysts and fund managers also use meetings with management to form impressions of management capabilities, and to gauge attitudes towards outside shareholders.

Because of asymmetries in the accessibility and interpretation of transnational accounting information, fund managers are heavily dependent on locally-based investment analysts, who are perceived to have the necessary expertise to deal with the relevant accounting and financial reporting systems. When analysing overseas equities, fund managers consider locally-based analysts' reports to be the most useful information source after direct company contact and accounting information. Furthermore, fund managers rely on these analysts to provide interpretation and analysis of foreign accounting information. This finding is important because Miles and Nobes (1998) state that UK fund managers think that analysts adjust accounting information, but the analysts in Miles and Nobes' study (i.e., analysts based in the UK) generally did not. The results of the current research indicate that the adjustments are more likely to be conducted by analysts based overseas.

Notwithstanding their use of overseas analysts, fund managers expressed reservations about analysts' independence due to a reluctance to jeopardise the analyst/manager relationship. Many fund managers therefore view analysts' recommendations with a degree of scepticism in light of a perceived reluctance to issue recommendations which reflect negatively on company management. Fund managers therefore face a dilemma in relying on sell-side analysts. They clearly need analysts as a link to management, to interpret foreign accounting information and as a means to overcome information asymmetries. Yet perceptions of bias in recommendations on company shares undermine fund managers' confidence in analyst independence. It should be noted, however, that the concerns related specifically to analysts' recommendations, rather than to the integrity of analysts' research in general. Moreover, as fund managers seem to be aware of potential conflicts, and if these problems are systematic, fund managers should be able to incorporate such factors into their decision making. Prior research supports this view (Dugar and Nathan, 1995).

The evidence on international variation in the usefulness of overseas information sources is mixed. In line with prior research (Choi and Levich, 1991), Swiss, German and Japanese accounting principles were identified in the interviews as being areas of concern. However, since the current research was conducted, some improvements have been made in these countries, such as requiring consolidated financial statements and better pension liabilities disclosures in Japan (Seki, 2000). Moreover, German companies will shortly be required to comply with IAS, along with other European countries.

Numerous comments in the interviews revealed some difficulties in obtaining the most basic of information sources such as the annual report, particularly for emerging markets. This reinforces assertions in prior research that information asymmetries between local and foreign investors exist, and may be responsible for impeding international capital flows (e.g., Gehrig, 1993; Kang and Stulz, 1997). Potentially, such information asymmetries have interesting financial implications for overseas equity analysis and they are worthy of future research. A comparison of investment performance in light of these asymmetries may indicate whether overseas investors are at a comparative disadvantage relative to domestic investors. Interestingly, Coval and Moskowitz (2001) find a relationship between geography and investment performance in a domestic context in the US. More specifically, they find that fund managers generate higher returns for local investments (i.e., within 100 kilometres of fund headquarters). They also call for research to investigate whether this phenomenon holds in an international context.

A final point on the use of transnational information is that the pace of change in information technology and the internet is causing changes in financial reporting. Although web-sites are regarded as more useful in foreign company analysis, they were not considered particularly influential in the questionnaire survey. In the interviews, however, there was a substantial improvement in perceptions of the internet, despite some criticisms being made of reliability of the information released on web-sites. Fund managers predicted a diminishing role for some analysts as a result of this technology. Further research will be necessary to keep track of the usefulness of web-sites and similar technology.

10.2.3 Harmonisation and international accounting differences

The results of the study do not support the idea that fund managers and analysts view international variation in accounting and financial reporting as a significant impediment in transnational analysis. The number of respondents who stated that international accounting differences have any serious effects on their decision making was relatively low. While previous research indicates that international accounting differences do have effects on cross-border decision making (Choi and Levich, 1991; Marton, 1998; Miles and Nobes, 1998), the results in this book appear to suggest that these effects are falling over time. The fact that financial institutions are becoming organised along sectoral rather than geographic lines is also indicative of international accounting differences having diminishing effects.

The description of information flows developed following analysis of survey results and interviews helps to explain these findings. While accounting information is considered very useful, it is not used in isolation. Fund managers are apparently mitigating the impact of international accounting differences by supplementing accounting information with discussions with company management, and by relying on local analysts for interpretative and analytical expertise. In addition, fund managers also correspond with UK-based institutional sales personnel, who also communicate frequently with locally-based analysts. Thus, non-comparable and potentially unfamiliar financial statement information is augmented by information from company management and interpretation from investment analysts.

A further potential explanation of why analysts and fund managers do not view themselves as being significantly affected by international accounting differences is that they apply a risk premium to allow for additional risk where they lack confidence in, or are unfamiliar with, certain foreign accounting standards. Both analysts and fund managers pointed out that foreign companies not reporting under IAS or US GAAP in certain markets have a significant premium attached to their discount rate. This represents a significant incentive for companies to attract foreign investors by reporting under accounting standards which are more familiar and more comparable internationally. In so doing, *ceteris paribus*, they are likely to increase demand for their shares and should see a reduction in their cost of equity capital.

These findings are in accordance with Glaum (2000), who found that the use of German accounting standards reduces demand for German shares overseas relative to IAS, and with Aggarwal *et al.* (2004), who find that the use of IAS or US GAAP is positively associated with US institutional investment in overseas firms. These results also provide supporting evidence of what Marton (1998) refers to as 'accounting risk', i.e., a risk premium demanded by investors for the additional 'noise' with which accounting numbers measure underlying economic variables. In order to fully assess the extent to which this effect can be reduced by improving the quality of accounting information, further investigation is needed into the extent to which this premium reflects 'actual' or 'perceived' (i.e., dependent on investors' perceptions of the quality of foreign accounting data) accounting risk. Given the strong support for harmonisation in the current research, it seems reasonable to infer that analysts and fund managers are reassured by the use of IAS/US GAAP. Hence, preparation of financial statements according to these standards looks likely to affect the risk premium, irrespective of whether these are actually objectively 'better' accounting standards.

The implications of this are wide ranging for the international accounting harmonisation debate. By offering the incentive of cheaper capital, the investment community appears able to influence the number of companies reporting under globally recognisable accounting standards such as IAS or US GAAP. By establishing a set of apparently reliable and politically acceptable global accounting standards, the IASB is providing a facility for companies world-wide to adopt standards which satisfy the needs of the international financial community. It is therefore not strictly necessary for the IASB to have enforcement powers to influence companies' decisions to adopt IAS. Provided that investors remain confident in the standards promulgated by the IASB, a powerful incentive exists for capital issuers to prepare their financial statements under these standards.

Given the view that international accounting differences do not materially affect fund managers' and analysts' decision making, one may reasonably expect a degree of indifference about international accounting harmonisation. However, somewhat paradoxically, the results demonstrate ubiquitous support for harmonisation among the fund managers and investment analysts. There is thus no evidence that either fund managers or investment analysts subordinate the harmonisation issue to the protection of their self interest.

Investigation of why support for harmonisation exists revealed that international comparability of financial information is highly important, especially for fund managers. Indeed, analysts and fund managers who compare financial statements internationally are significantly more supportive of harmonisation. Comparability is likely to remain an important issue as financial institutions shift to a sectoral versus country-based specialism. However, comparability is not the only determinant of support for harmonisation. Some comments from fund managers suggested that adoption of globally recognisable accounting standards also acts as a signal to analysts and fund managers that companies are attuned to the needs of equity investors. This indicates that the preference for IAS and US GAAP is not simply a product of perceived superior quality of accounting standards. Recognisable accounting standards such as IAS and US GAAP signify a 'shareholder-friendly' attitude, irrespective of the 'quality' of accounting standards. Finally, there does not appear to be any preference over whether IAS or US GAAP are ultimately adopted. Thus, consistent with the findings of Marton (1998) and Leuz (2003), the issue that *one* set of standards is applied is far more important than *which* set of standards is applied.

10.2.4 Limitations of the empirical study

When interpreting the findings of the current research, a number of potential methodological limitations should be considered. The first relates to the number and proportion of analysts and fund managers responding to the questionnaire. Although the sample size and response rate are comparable with previous published research, it cannot be conclusively proven that the findings of the questionnaire survey are representative of the population of UK analysts and fund managers.

The findings of the interviews, although more detailed and comprehensive than the questionnaire survey, may also not be generalisable to the population of UK-based analysts and fund managers. This is one of the key limitations of conducting interview-based research in general, as the sample size can be constrained by costs, time and/or the number of individuals willing and able to participate in the research. However, as shown in the Appendix, the participants in the interviews comprised a mix of fund managers and investment analysts covering various industrial sectors and geographic regions, including Europe, North and South America, Japan, Asia and emerging markets.

A further possible limitation is that the results may not be generalisable beyond the UK, as Arnold *et al.* (1984) and Marton (1998) found that the investment approaches and information sources used by analysts vary depending on their location and environment. Therefore, it is possible that analysts and fund managers based outside the UK adopt different approaches to analysing overseas shares and have different attitudes to harmonisation than UK-based fund managers and analysts.

Finally, it is worth pointing out that through the employment of two complementary methods of data collection and analysis, the problems associated with one individual approach may be reduced (Jick, 1979). The broad consistency between the interview and questionnaire results in the areas that overlapped provides some reassurance of the validity of the findings of the research.

10.3 CONCLUDING REMARKS

Overall, this book may be seen as a response to contentions that the perspectives of analysts and fund managers have been neglected in prior research into transnational financial decisions, and that transnational information processing is poorly understood (e.g., Hopwood, 1994).

The book has shown that despite significant international differences in accounting and financial reporting, accounting information and accounting-based analysis techniques are as useful to institutional users in overseas company analysis as they are in domestic company analysis. Indeed, provided it is available to overseas investors (particularly when translated into English), the annual report and the financial statements are essential information sources.

The book has also provided explanations for why accounting data is so valuable, and how analysts and particularly fund managers overcome international accounting and financial reporting differences. *Inter alia*, they use measures for valuation which are more comparable across national boundaries. Additionally, a partial solution to the problem of the incomparability of international accounting information is the active market in the interpretation and analysis of financial statement data provided by locally-based analysts.

A further information source used to augment accounting information is direct personal contact with company management. Local analysts are also useful to fund managers in gaining access to company management, although the analyst/manager relationship is a matter of some concern to some fund managers, especially in the context of share recommendations, which fund managers see as overly optimistic.

The book also provides evidence on the support from analysts and fund managers for international accounting harmonisation, and mechanisms for dealing with the diversity in national financial reporting systems. The findings show that where international accounting differences cannot be directly overcome by dependence on local expertise or company personnel, fund managers and analysts allow for increased uncertainty by incorporating a risk premium into their decisions. By doing so, they encourage companies to report under accounting standards which are comparable and familiar to fund managers with significant equity funds at their disposal.

In addition to the regulatory efforts made to improve international comparability of accounting information by the IASB, it therefore appears that additional forces are also at work. *Prima facie*, competitive capital markets are apparently helping to ensure that international accounting differences and financial reporting differences are not an insurmountable impediment to cross-border investment.

10.4 REFERENCES

Aggarwal, R., Klapper, L. and Wysocki, P.D. (2004). 'Portfolio preferences of foreign institutional investors.' *MIT Sloan School of Management Working Paper*.

Arnold, J., Moizer, P. and Noreen, E. (1984). 'Investment appraisal methods of financial analysts: a comparative study of US and UK practices.' *International Journal of Accounting*, **Spring**, 1–18.

Barker, R.G. (2001). *Institutional Investors, Accounting Information and the ASB*. Institute of Charted Accountants of Scotland, Edinburgh.

Charitou, A. and Edwards, K.J. (1990). 'Valuation of earnings, cash flows and their components: an empirical investigation.' *Journal of Accounting, Auditing and Finance*, **5**, (4), 475–497.

Choi, F.D.S. and Levich, R.M. (1991). 'Behavioral effects of international accounting diversity.' *Accounting Horizons*, **June**, 1–13.

Coval, J.D. and Moskowitz, T.J. (2001). 'The geography of investment: informed trading and asset prices.' *Journal of Political Economy*, **109** (4), 811–841.

Davies, M., Paterson, R. and Wilson, A. (1999). *UK GAAP*, 6th edn, Ernst and Young, London.

Dugar, A. and Nathan, S. (1995). 'The effect of investment banking relationships on financial analysts' earnings forecasts and investment recommendations.' *Contemporary Accounting Research*, **12** (1), 131–160.

Francis, J., Schipper, K. and Vincent, L. (2003). 'The relative incremental explanatory power of earnings and alternative (to earnings) performance measures for returns.' *Contemporary Accounting Research*, **20** (1), 121–164.

Gehrig, T. (1993). 'An information based explanation of the domestic bias in international equity investment.' *Scandinavian Journal of Economics*, **95** (1), 97–109.

Glaum, M. (2000). 'Bridging the GAAP: the changing attitudes of German managers towards Anglo-American accounting and accounting harmonisation.' *Journal of International Financial Management and Accounting*, **11** (1), 23–47.

Hopwood, A.G. (1994). 'Some reflections on "The Harmonization of Accounting Within the EU".' *The European Accounting Review*, **3** (2), 241–253.

Jick, T.D. (1979). 'Mixing qualitative and quantitative methods: triangulation in action.' *Administrative Science Quarterly*, **24**, 602–611.

Kang, J. and Stulz, R.M. (1997). 'Why is there a home-bias? An analysis of foreign portfolio equity ownership in Japan.' *Journal of Financial Economics*, **46**, 3–28.

Leuz, C. (2003). 'IAS versus US GAAP: information-asymmetry based evidence from Germany's new market.' *Journal of Accounting Research*, **41**, 445–472.

Marton, J. (1998). *Accounting and Stock Markets: A Study of Swedish Accounting for International Investors and Analysts*, BAS, Gothenburg University, Sweden.

Miles, S. and Nobes, C. (1998). 'The use of foreign accounting data in UK financial institutions.' *Journal of Business Finance and Accounting*, **25** (3 and 4), 309–328.

Olbert, L. (1994). 'Stock valuation methods of financial analysts in a thin stock market in Sweden, with comparisons to the United Kingdom and the United States.' *International Journal of Accounting*, **29**, 123–135.

Seki, M. (2000). 'Reshaping standards.' *Accountancy*, **June**, 110.

Appendix

DETAILS OF INTERVIEW RESPONDENTS

	Gender	Description	Employer
Analyst 1	M	Sell-side analyst specialising in European construction companies	American controlled investment bank in London
Analyst 2	M	Director of European equities	French controlled investment bank in London
Analyst 3	M	Sell-side analyst specialising in European telecoms companies	German controlled investment bank in London
Analyst 4	M	Buy-side analyst and strategist specialising in European insurance companies	UK insurance company in London
Analyst 5	M	Sell-side analyst specialising in European leisure and hotel companies	French controlled investment bank in London
Analyst 6	M	Sell-side analyst specialising in European pharmaceutical companies	French controlled investment bank in London
Analyst 7	M	Buy-side analyst and strategist specialising in global cyclical equities	Swiss controlled investment bank in London
Analyst 8	M	Director of emerging European equities	Swiss controlled investment bank in London
Analyst 9	M	Sell-side analyst specialising in European steel companies	American controlled investment bank in London

Continued

Continued

	Gender	Description	Employer
Analyst 10	M	Sell-side (institutional sales) analyst specialising in US equities	American controlled stockbroker in London
Analyst 11	M	Sell-side (institutional sales) analyst specialising in Japanese equities	American controlled investment bank in London
FM 1	M	Manager of Asian and Japanese fund	UK institutional investor in London
FM 2	M	Manager of Japanese fund	UK institutional investor in London
FM 3	M	Asset allocator for Emerging markets	German controlled institutional investor in London
FM 4	M	Manager of US small company fund	UK institutional investor in London
FM 5	M	Manager of US fund	UK institutional investor in Oxford
FM 6	M	Manager of European fund (specialising in oils, services and biotech)	American controlled institutional investor in London
FM 7	M	Manager of Asian fund	UK institutional investor in London
FM 8	M	Manager of European fund	UK institutional investor in London
FM 9	F	Manager of European small company fund	UK institutional investor in London
FM 10	M	Manager of emerging markets fund	UK institutional investor in London
FM 11	M	Manager of European fund (specialising in banks)	UK institutional investor in London
FM 12	M	Manager of Pacific Asia fund specialising in global autos, internet and tech companies)	UK institutional investor in London
FM 13	M	Manager of Japanese fund	UK institutional investor in Edinburgh
FM 14	M	Manager of Japanese fund	UK institutional investor in London
FM 15	M	Manager of Latin America fund	Australian controlled institutional investor in London
FM 16	M	Manager of Japanese fund (specialising in technology companies)	American controlled institutional investor in London

Continued

Continued

	Gender	Description	Employer
FM 17	F	Manager of US small company fund	UK institutional investor in London
FM 18	M	Director of international fund management	UK institutional investor in Edinburgh
FM 19	M	Manager of Japanese fund	UK institutional investor in London
FM 20	M	Director of European institutional investment	UK institutional investor in London

Index